WORD SEARCHES

for cleVer Kids

Buster Books

Puzzles and solutions created
by Gareth Moore

Illustrations by Chris Dickason

Edited by Lauren Farnsworth

Cover design by Angie Allison

First published in Great Britain in 2015 by Buster Books,
an imprint of Michael O'Mara Books Limited,
9 Lion Yard, Tremadoc Road, London SW4 7NQ

W   www.busterbooks.co.uk

f   Buster Children's Books

🐦   @BusterBooks

A CIP catalogue record for this book is available from the British Library.

ISBN: 978-1-78055-307-8

2 4 6 8 10 9 7 5 3

Papers used by Buster Books are natural, recyclable products
made from wood grown in sustainable forests. The manufacturing processes
conform to the environmental regulations of the country of origin.

Printed and bound in March 2016 by CPI Group
(UK) Ltd, Croydon, CR0 4YY

INTRODUCTION

Wordsearches are the perfect challenge for seriously clever kids. This book contains over a thousand words to spot in over 160 puzzles. The puzzles are divided into four levels of difficulty, and get tougher as the book progresses.

Beneath each puzzle grid you'll see a list of words that you must find. Don't worry if you don't know what all the words mean because you can still spot them. Words may be hidden in the grids in any direction, including diagonally, and may run either forwards or backwards. Some of the words might even overlap and use the same letters.

When you find a word, mark it with a pen, pencil or highlighter and then cross it off the list. If you get stuck on any word, the answers are all at the back of the book, so you can take a sneak peak if you need to.

Some of the puzzles might contain a phrase or a word written with punctuation or spaces. In these cases, just ignore the spaces or punctuation marks when searching, and only search for the letters. There are also some interestingly shaped puzzles with lines drawn between the letters in the grid. When you come across one of these, ignore the lines, as the words can still run across them.

There's a 'Time' line at the top of every page for you to write in how long it took you to do each puzzle.

PUZZLE 1: FLOWERS

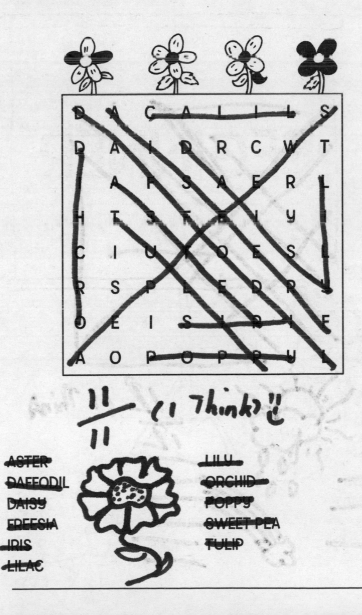

11/11 (I Think) ♔

ASTER
DAFFODIL
DAISY
FREESIA
IRIS
LILAC

LILU
ORCHID
POPPY
SWEET PEA
TULIP

BEGINNER

Time ....

PUZZLE 2: WEATHER

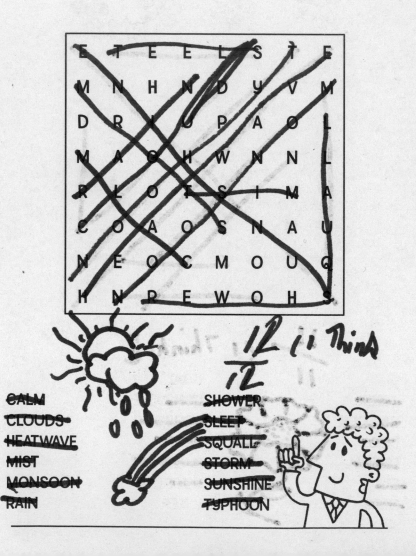

E	T	E	E	L	S	T	E	E
M	N	H	N	D	Y	V	M	
D	R	I	U	P	A	O	L	
M	A	C	H	W	N	N	L	
R	L	O	T	S	I	M	A	
C	O	A	O	S	N	A	U	
N	E	O	C	M	O	U	Q	
K	N	R	E	W	O	H	S	

CALM
CLOUDS
HEATWAVE
MIST
MONSOON
RAIN

SHOWER
SLEET
SQUALL
STORM
SUNSHINE
TYPHOON

PUZZLE 3: FARM ANIMALS

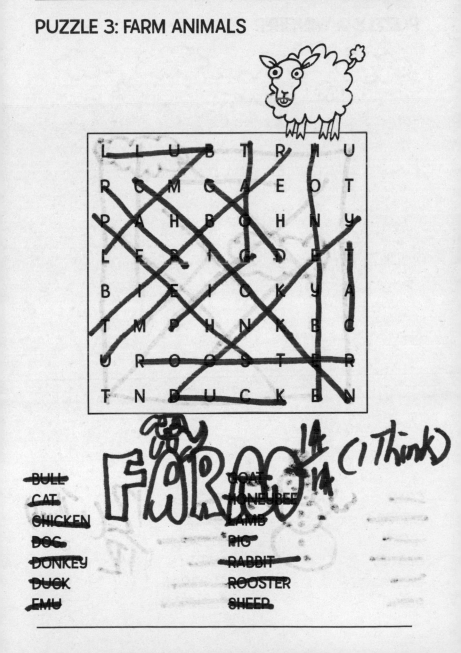

L	I	U	B	T	R	M	U
R	C	M	G	A	E	O	T
P	A	H	B	O	H	N	Y
L	E	R	C	G	D	E	T
B	I	E	I	C	K	Y	A
T	M	P	H	N	K	B	C
U	R	O	O	S	T	E	R
T	N	D	U	C	K	E	N

~~BULL~~   ~~GOAT~~
~~CAT~~   ~~HONEYBEE~~
~~CHICKEN~~   ~~LAMB~~
~~DOG~~   ~~PIG~~
~~DONKEY~~   ~~RABBIT~~
~~DUCK~~   ROOSTER
~~EMU~~   ~~SHEEP~~

PUZZLE 4: WINTER

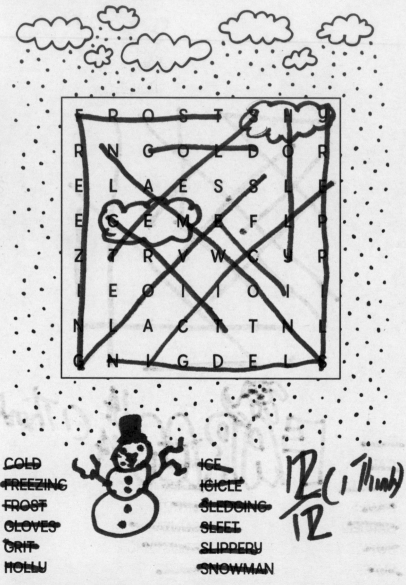

F R O S T I N G
R N G O L D O R
E L A E S S L E
E G E M E F L P
Z T R W C Y P
L E O I O N I
N L A C T N L
G N I G D E L S

COLD   ICE
FREEZING   ICICLE
FROST   SLEDGING
GLOVES   SLEET
GRIT   SLIPPERY
HOLLY   SNOWMAN

PUZZLE 5: SUMMER

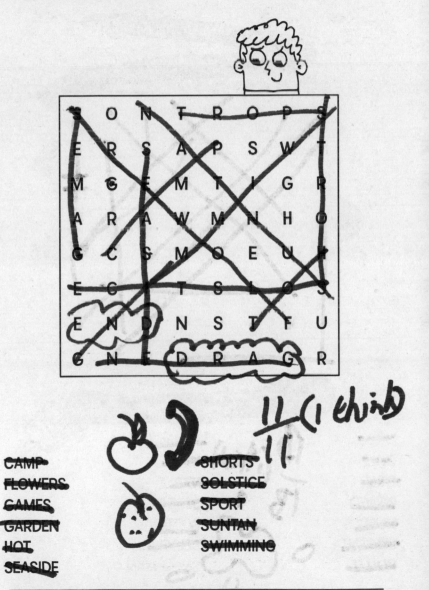

S	O	N	T	R	O	P	S
E	R	S	A	P	S	W	T
M	G	E	M	T	I	G	R
A	R	A	W	M	N	H	O
C	C	S	M	O	E	U	H
E	E	I	T	S	L	O	S
E	N	D	N	S	T	F	U
G	N	E	D	R	A	G	R

CAMP
FLOWERS
GAMES
GARDEN
HOT
SEASIDE

SHORTS
SOLSTICE
SPORT
SUNTAN
SWIMMING

BEGINNER

 Time ....

PUZZLE 6: COLOURS

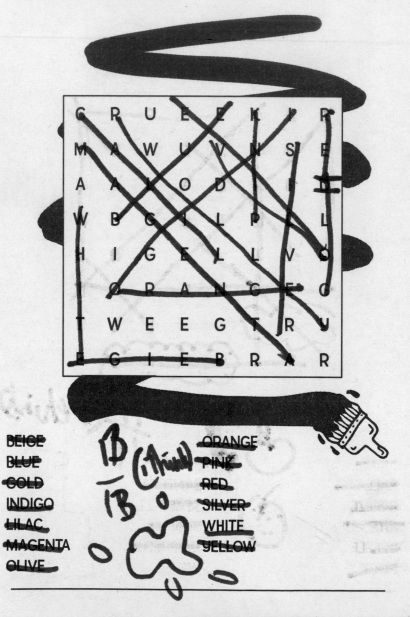

```
C R U E E K I R
M A W U V N S E
A A K O D I I E
W B C I L P L L
H I G E L L V O
I O R A N G E C
T W E E G T R V
E E G I E B R A R
```

BEIGE
BLUE
GOLD
INDIGO
LILAC
MAGENTA
OLIVE

ORANGE
PINK
RED
SILVER
WHITE
YELLOW

PUZZLE 7: AT THE BEACH

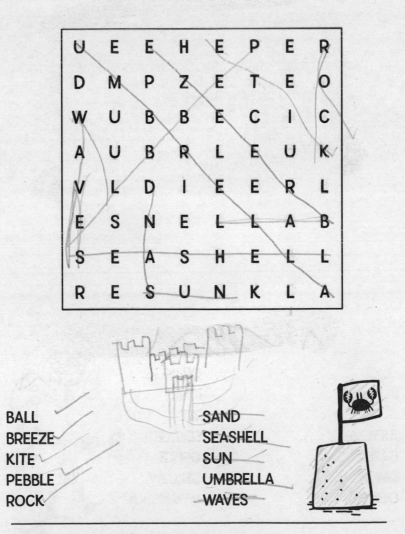

U	E	E	H	E	P	E	R
D	M	P	Z	E	T	E	O
W	U	B	B	E	C	I	C
A	U	B	R	L	E	U	K
V	L	D	I	E	E	R	L
E	S	N	E	L	L	A	B
S	E	A	S	H	E	L	L
R	E	S	U	N	K	L	A

BALL
BREEZE
KITE
PEBBLE
ROCK

SAND
SEASHELL
SUN
UMBRELLA
WAVES

BEGINNER   Time ....

PUZZLE 8: SCHOOL

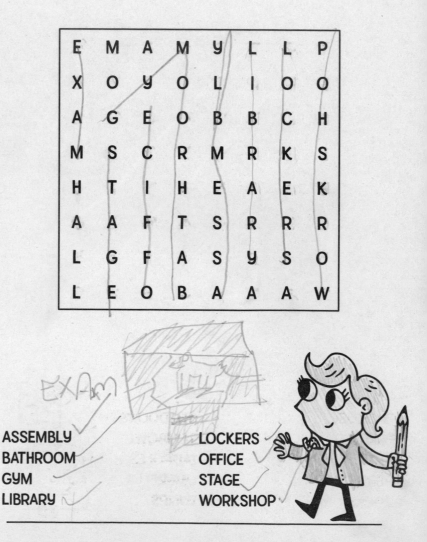

E	M	A	M	Y	L	L	P
X	O	Y	O	L	I	O	O
A	G	E	O	B	B	C	H
M	S	C	R	M	R	K	S
H	T	I	H	E	A	E	K
A	A	F	T	S	R	R	R
L	G	F	A	S	Y	S	O
L	E	O	B	A	A	A	W

ASSEMBLY
BATHROOM
GYM
LIBRARY

LOCKERS
OFFICE
STAGE
WORKSHOP

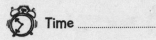

PUZZLE 9: SPRING

```
T  A  D  P  O  L  O  E  S
S  P  I  L  U  T  W  E
O  U  T  D  O  O  R  S
T  L  I  H  B  B  E  U
E  A  A  N  A  V  T  C
O  G  I  M  A  W  S  O
L  A  G  E  B  E  A  R
R  A  L  S  U  S  E  C
```

CROCUSES   OUTDOORS
EASTER   RAINBOWS
EGGS   TADPOLES
LAMBS   THAW
LEAVES   TULIPS

PUZZLE 10: AUTUMN

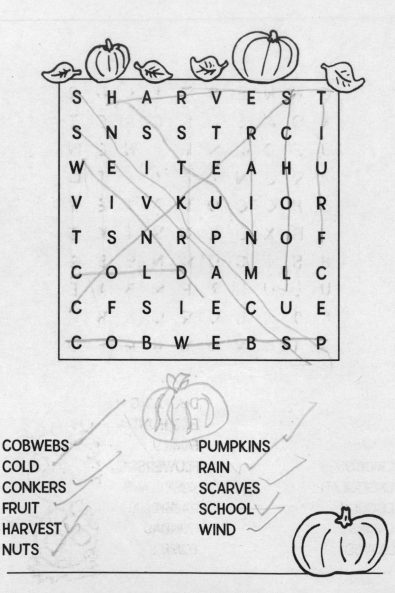

```
S  H  A  R  V  E  S  T
S  N  S  S  T  R  C  I
W  E  I  T  E  A  H  U
V  I  V  K  U  I  O  R
T  S  N  R  P  N  O  F
C  O  L  D  A  M  L  C
C  F  S  I  E  C  U  E
C  O  B  W  E  B  S  P
```

COBWEBS   PUMPKINS
COLD   RAIN
CONKERS   SCARVES
FRUIT   SCHOOL
HARVEST   WIND
NUTS

PUZZLE 11: EASTER

```
C F N E S T T L D R
H D A S O E C A G T
U E O M N H F N G N
R R B N I F I E T U
C H O C O L A T E H
H B K D K O Y I K G
H S I C D W N B S G
U L U L T E N B A E
S D N B O R U A B O
Y A D N U S B R F D
```

BASKET
BONNET
BUNNY
CHICKS
CHOCOLATE
CHURCH
CROSS
DAFFODILS

DUCKLING
EGG HUNT
FAMILY
FLOWERS
NEST
RABBIT
SUNDAY
TOMB

PUZZLE 12: TRAVEL

```
L A V I R R A P N E
D P N S E P L I X T
R A A R G A K C O A
I C A M N C U U L K
V K N N E R R U S E
I I I H S I G T E O
N N C I S G R T T F
G G O M A I U I O F
G N O G P O J I F M
U Y E N R U O J F N
```

ARRIVAL
CHECK-IN
DRIVING
EXCURSION
JOURNEY
LUGGAGE
MAP
PACKING

PASSENGER
PLANNING
ROUTE
SET OFF
TAKE OFF
TOURISM
TRIP

PUZZLE 13: IN THE GARDEN

R	G	R	W	R	M	R	I	E	H
E	E	W	E	O	S	P	E	S	S
L	V	R	W	N	A	B	G	U	E
K	I	E	R	V	U	A	S	N	E
N	R	G	I	S	Z	R	W	B	R
I	D	N	H	E	E	A	P	A	T
R	G	U	B	W	L	V	U	T	V
P	G	O	O	S	R	I	A	H	C
S	E	L	B	A	T	E	G	E	V
O	F	B	S	H	R	U	B	A	L

BUSH	MOWER
CHAIRS	PAVING
DRIVE	PRUNER
FLOWERS	SHRUB
GAZEBO	SPRINKLER
LAWN	SUNBATHE
LEAVES	TREES
LOUNGER	VEGETABLES

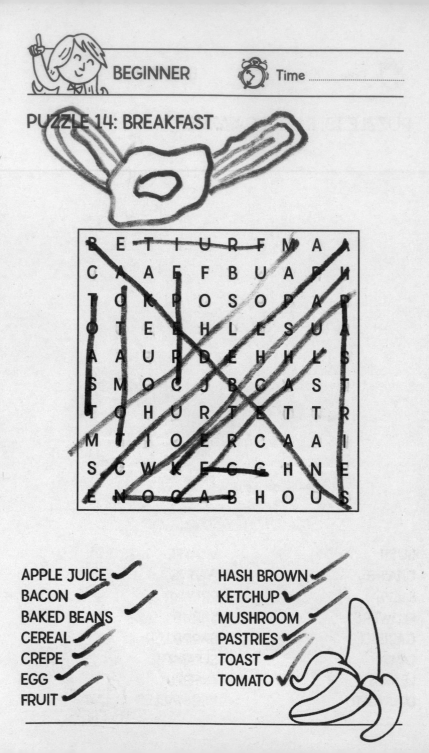

PUZZLE 14: BREAKFAST

```
R E T I U R F M A A
C A A F F B U A P H
T O K P O S O P A R
O T E L H L E S U A
A A U R D E H H L S
S M O C J B C A S T
T O H U R T E T T R
M T I O E R C A A I
S C W K F E G G H N E
E N O C A B H O U S
```

APPLE JUICE
BACON
BAKED BEANS
CEREAL
CREPE
EGG
FRUIT

HASH BROWN
KETCHUP
MUSHROOM
PASTRIES
TOAST
TOMATO

PUZZLE 15: SEVEN DWARVES

P	S	G	L	E	L	A	P	O	E
Y	H	E	S	M	Y	L	F	N	Y
O	Z	O	Y	P	M	U	R	G	L
R	Y	E	P	O	D	Y	M	U	U
C	A	A	E	E	O	L	F	P	H
P	H	Y	E	N	C	H	F	P	Y
E	O	O	L	Y	S	Y	L	D	Y
B	O	L	S	A	P	S	E	L	O
R	C	P	B	G	E	Z	H	Y	Y
U	S	Y	L	H	E	O	S	L	B

BASHFUL   HAPPY
DOC   SLEEPY
DOPEY   SNEEZY
GRUMPY

PUZZLE 16: PRECIOUS METALS

P	A	L	L	A	D	I	U	M	U
M	M	U	H	M	M	N	E	U	R
M	U	I	D	O	H	R	R	N	U
O	I	I	M	I	C	E	M	I	H
H	D	M	L	U	V	U	D	T	P
O	I	I	R	L	I	M	U	A	L
I	R	Y	I	U	A	M	L	L	R
L	I	S	L	H	S	G	S	P	I
I	U	M	G	I	G	D	L	O	G
T	L	L	B	S	E	M	B	N	I

BISMUTH   OSMIUM
GALLIUM   PALLADIUM
GOLD   PLATINUM
IRIDIUM   RHODIUM
MERCURY   SILVER

PUZZLE 17: BAKING EQUIPMENT

N	R	S	E	L	D	A	L	T	S
A	O	E	W	F	D	N	A	K	S
N	L	O	N	H	I	S	E	S	I
O	L	M	P	I	S	N	E	I	S
U	I	B	L	S	A	L	K	H	P
U	N	R	E	T	A	R	G	W	A
T	G	E	A	C	E	E	T	L	T
W	P	L	S	X	R	N	T	S	U
M	I	X	I	N	G	B	O	W	L
L	N	M	L	L	L	K	E	O	A

GRATER   SCALES
KNIFE   SPATULA
LADLE   STRAINER
MIXER   TEASPOON
MIXING BOWL   WHISK
ROLLING PIN

BEGINNER Time ....

PUZZLE 18: SLEEPING

```
G W O R N O U T Z E
H N C G N I T S E R
E D I D V T X X G G
A O G R I R H U N N
V Z R O E A S I I I
Y I A W U B P E P Z
E N H S E P M T E O
Y G T Y A A I U E O
E E E N O N R D L N
D I L A T G G Y S S
```

DOZING	RESTING
DROWSY	SLEEPING
EXHAUSTED	SLUMBERING
HEAVY-EYED	SNOOZING
LETHARGIC	WEARY
NAPPING	WORN OUT

PUZZLE 19: NOISE

N	O	I	T	A	R	B	I	V	A
T	K	D	C	P	C	H	I	M	E
R	N	T	E	P	A	U	R	T	R
S	O	T	R	L	L	N	E	E	O
D	C	A	H	A	B	L	K	K	N
N	K	R	E	U	T	M	E	C	S
U	H	U	E	S	N	T	U	A	I
O	Q	U	I	E	S	D	L	R	R
S	N	H	N	D	C	A	E	E	E
U	W	G	N	A	B	H	B	R	N

APPLAUSE   SCREECH
BANG   SIREN
BASS   SNORE
CHIME   SOUND
KNOCK   SQUEAL
RACKET   THUNDER
RATTLE   VIBRATION
RUMBLE   WHISTLE

PUZZLE 20: JUNGLE

```
S  F  T  F  E  M  A  C  F  F
V  E  S  H  L  E  S  R  E  O
R  S  R  E  G  O  U  S  R  R
S  D  N  U  N  I  W  S  S  E
E  R  E  P  T  I  L  E  S  S
V  A  E  S  C  A  V  N  R  T
A  Z  S  D  M  N  N  K  U  S
E  I  E  I  I  B  I  R  D  S
L  L  N  Z  A  P  N  A  T  O
C  A  N  O  P  Y  S  D  R  M
```

ANIMALS	LIZARDS
BIRDS	MOSS
CANOPY	NATURE
DARKNESS	RAIN
FLOWERS	REPTILES
FOREST	SPIDERS
FRUIT	SUNLIGHT
LEAVES	VINES

PUZZLE 21: OWLS

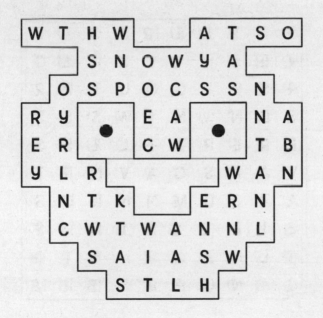

BARN
HAWK
LITTLE

SCOPS
SNOWY
TAWNY

PUZZLE 22: UNDER THE BED

```
S S B M U R C T U P
O H T S S O O N M E
H O S I R Y D O G G
I K T U S E N D A A
P A P E R S D U C R
C A O W T B U I E O
U H E E S I R E P T
S A R B B G C I S S
R S E N I Z A G A M
S S O C K S E B B H
```

BAGS	PAPERS
CAT	SHOES
CRUMBS	SOCKS
DOG	SPIDERS
HAIRBRUSH	STORAGE
MAGAZINES	TOYS
MONSTERS	UNDERWEAR

PUZZLE 23: CONTINENTS

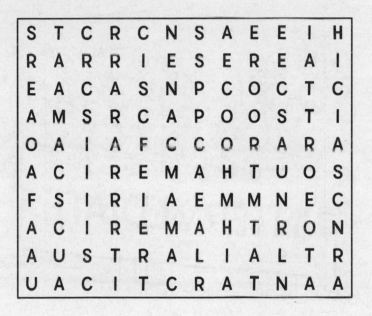

S	T	C	R	C	N	S	A	E	E	I	H
R	A	R	R	I	E	S	E	R	E	A	I
E	A	C	A	S	N	P	C	O	C	T	C
A	M	S	R	C	A	P	O	O	S	T	I
O	A	I	A	F	C	C	O	R	A	R	A
A	C	I	R	E	M	A	H	T	U	O	S
F	S	I	R	I	A	E	M	M	N	E	C
A	C	I	R	E	M	A	H	T	R	O	N
A	U	S	T	R	A	L	I	A	L	T	R
U	A	C	I	T	C	R	A	T	N	A	A

AFRICA

ANTARCTICA

ASIA

AUSTRALIA

EUROPE

NORTH AMERICA

SOUTH AMERICA

PUZZLE 24: SAFARI ANIMALS

```
C H G A R B E Z L U G H
C U C I W L U N G N A I
A A R I R I N F O A Z P
L A R H R A L P F I E P
A O N A I T F D A A L O
P H R E C N S F D G L P
M A A Y Y A O O E O E O
I U P T X H L C O H G T
      E P O L E T N A
      L E O P A R D M
      R L H A R A O U
      A E H C L W I S
```

ANTELOPE
BUFFALO
CARACAL
CHEETAH
ELEPHANT
GAZELLE
GIRAFFE
GNU
HIPPOPOTAMUS
HYENA

IMPALA
LEOPARD
LION
ORYX
OSTRICH
RHINOCEROS
WARTHOG
WILD DOG
ZEBRA

PUZZLE 25: PIRATES

I	N	W	C	K	N	S	M	K	L	U	H
E	S	W	A	N	N	A	G	L	N	G	S
E	W	W	P	S	D	E	A	R	B	N	A
B	O	P	T	J	O	B	A	L	W	N	W
W	R	E	A	E	N	F	A	C	O	D	G
L	C	C	I	O	L	C	I	T	R	G	U
E	K	G	N	I	K	E	T	A	R	I	P
C	C	N	N	B	T	O	E	G	A	K	O
K	A	T	E	U	N	B	O	M	P	H	P
C	J	A	M	D	D	A	M	H	S	I	A
C	R	I	O	E	T	T	I	F	A	L	I
D	N	D	R	A	E	B	K	N	U	K	S

BLACKBEARD	PIRATE KING
CANNONBALL	PUGWASH
CAPTAIN NEMO	REDBEARD
FLINT	SKUNKBEARD
HOOK	SMEE
JACK CROW	SPARROW
LAFITTE	SWANN
MAD JACK	

PUZZLE 26: COUNTRIES

```
N N L I T H U A N I A A
I O S S E W B A B M I Z
C S W I T Z E R L A N D
A A A N I N E B U D A N
R F Z G         X A T A
A A I A         E G S L
G N L P         M A H N
U I A O         B S K E
A K N R I C Q U O C A E
R R D E I O C A U A Z R
S U R I N A M E R R A G
O B P O L A N D G I K I
```

BENIN
BURKINA FASO
CUBA
GREENLAND
IRAN
IRAQ
KAZAKHSTAN
LITHUANIA
LUXEMBOURG

MADAGASCAR
NICARAGUA
POLAND
SINGAPORE
SURINAME
SWAZILAND
SWITZERLAND
ZIMBABWE

PUZZLE 27: ICE-CREAM FLAVOURS

```
R B R P N I Y O R L E A
A C L N L C T C Y L G E
N A A O R E E O R C R M
A L O R A R E T C Y R V
O E Y A A T A E R Y A E
A V M E N M O R A N G E
A T C I G A E F I O A L
L C M T L H H L F M O P
A C H O C O L A T E I P
B A N A N A M H R L E A
A M T E A E E Y G C A C
C L Y A L H O H E A F R
```

APPLE   LEMON
BANANA   LIME
CARAMEL   MINT
CHERRY   ORANGE
CHOCOLATE   TOFFEE
HONEY   VANILLA

PUZZLE 28: HALLOWEEN

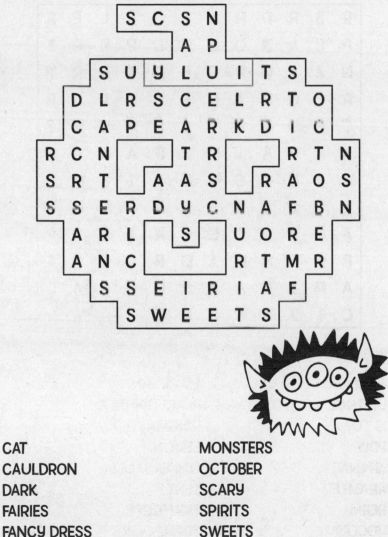

CAT	MONSTERS
CAULDRON	OCTOBER
DARK	SCARY
FAIRIES	SPIRITS
FANCY DRESS	SWEETS
LANTERNS	

PUZZLE 29: CIRCUS

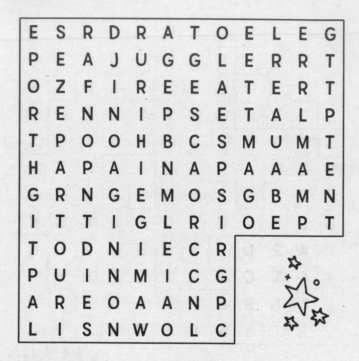

```
E S R D R A T O E L E G
P E A J U G G L E R R T
O Z F I R E E A T E R T
R E N N I P S E T A L P
T P O O H B C S M U M T
H A P A I N A P A A A E
G R N G E M O S G B M N
I T T I G L R I O E P T
T O D N I E C R
P U I N M I C G
A R E O A A N P
L I S N W O L C
```

ACROBAT	MAGICIAN
AUDIENCE	PLATE SPINNER
BIG TOP	RINGMASTER
CLOWN	SEAL
ELEPHANT	SOMERSAULT
FIRE-EATER	TENT
HOOP	TIGHTROPE
JUGGLER	TRAMPOLINE
LEOTARD	TRAPEZE

PUZZLE 30: CHRISTMAS

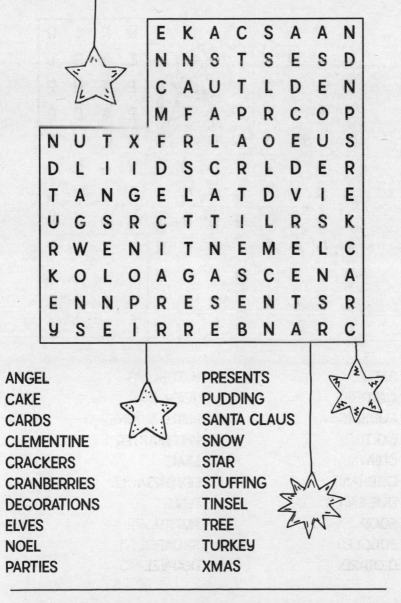

```
        E  K  A  C  S  A  A  N
        N  N  S  T  S  E  S  D
        C  A  U  T  L  D  E  N
        M  F  A  P  R  C  O  P
N  U  T  X  F  R  L  A  O  E  U  S
D  L  I  I  D  S  C  R  L  D  E  R
T  A  N  G  E  L  A  T  D  V  I  E
U  G  S  R  C  T  T  I  L  R  S  K
R  W  E  N  I  T  N  E  M  E  L  C
K  O  L  O  A  G  A  S  C  E  N  A
E  N  N  P  R  E  S  E  N  T  S  R
Y  S  E  I  R  R  E  B  N  A  R  C
```

ANGEL	PRESENTS
CAKE	PUDDING
CARDS	SANTA CLAUS
CLEMENTINE	SNOW
CRACKERS	STAR
CRANBERRIES	STUFFING
DECORATIONS	TINSEL
ELVES	TREE
NOEL	TURKEY
PARTIES	XMAS

PUZZLE 31: BABY ANIMALS

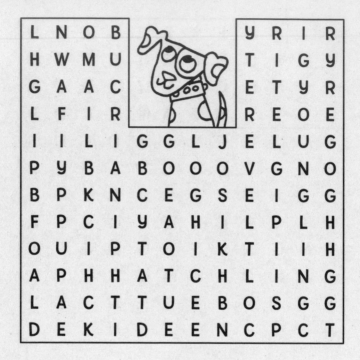

L	N	O	B				Y	R	I	R
H	W	M	U				T	I	G	Y
G	A	A	C				E	T	Y	R
L	F	I	R				R	E	O	E
I	I	L	I	G	G	L	J	E	L	U	G
P	Y	B	A	B	O	O	O	V	G	N	O
B	P	K	N	C	E	G	S	E	I	G	G
F	P	C	I	Y	A	H	I	L	P	L	H
O	U	I	P	T	O	I	K	T	I	I	H
A	P	H	H	A	T	C	H	L	I	N	G
L	A	C	T	T	U	E	B	O	S	G	G
D	E	K	I	D	E	E	N	C	P	C	T

BABY	HATCHLING
CALF	JOEY
CHICK	KID
COLT	KITTEN
CRIA	LAMB
CUB	LEVERET
DUCKLING	PIGLET
FAWN	PUPPY
FOAL	SHOAT
GOSLING	YOUNGLING

PUZZLE 32: WATERBIRDS

K	C	U	D	W	H	I	M	B	R	E	L
N	M	W	D	T	F	M	B	T	L	Y	M
T	O	N	R	L	S	I	U	U	R	E	R
E	O	T	I	I	T	R	N	E	T	N	S
F	R	M	B	T	N	I	H	T	N	E	S
P	H	I	E	S	L	S	S	I	A	D	O
L	E	R	T	L	I	E	E	W	R	L	R
O	N	O	A	F	L	P	A	E	O	O	T
V	N	G	G	L	S	I	G	E	M	G	A
E	S	N	I	L	W	N	U	P	R	I	B
R	I	A	R	B	A	S	L	G	O	M	L
K	R	C	F	A	N	W	L	H	C	A	A

ALBATROSS
BITTERN
CORMORANT
DUCK
FRIGATE BIRD
GALLINULE
GOLDENEYE
GUILLEMOT
IBIS
KINGFISHER

MOORHEN
PEEWIT
PLOVER
RAIL
SEAGULL
SNIPE
STILT
SWAN
TURNSTONE
WHIMBREL

PUZZLE 33: ANIMAL NOISES

```
P N R M L H C K
L N H U G W A N
E N T P C U O E
G A U P S S I H
R R L S N A P T K N R G
R E O O A L O C W R B G
Y T R W R O A R O A A K
U T N C L U C K E I A B
K A E U Q S U I M H N K
W H I N N Y E G R K B K
O C G O E Z Z U B R S N
A R H E N K R N N K A A
```

BAA	OINK
BARK	PURR
BUZZ	QUACK
CHATTER	ROAR
CLUCK	SNAP
GROWL	SNARL
HISS	SNORT
HOWL	SQUEAK
MEOW	WHINNY
NEIGH	YELP

PUZZLE 34: SWEETS

```
R E P P O T S B O G T E
L P I T A G U O N O R T
F O N D A N T A F U A T
P R U L O M E F T V E E
L D O B I B E X L Y C S
E N N E Y E I A E I U I
W O L L A M H S R A M O
B M L P Y E L O E E N N
B E P L R L U G
J L L O U Q D E
E O C B I U S B
D K L L F V O O
```

BONBON
BULL'S-EYE
DOLLY MIXTURE
FONDANT
FUDGE
GOBSTOPPER
HALVA
JELLY BEAN

LEMON DROP
LIQUORICE
MARSHMALLOW
NOISETTE
NOUGAT
ROCK
TOFFEE APPLE

PUZZLE 35: MONTHS OF THE YEAR

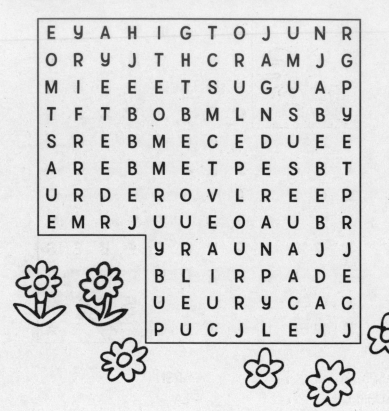

```
E Y A H I G T O J U N R
O R Y J T H C R A M J G
M I E E E T S U G U A P
T F T B O B M L N S B Y
S R E B M E C E D U E E
A R E B M E T P E S B T
U R D E R O V L R E E P
E M R J U U E O A U B R
        Y R A U N A J J
        B L I R P A D E
        U E U R Y C A C
        P U C J L E J J
```

APRIL   JUNE
AUGUST   MARCH
DECEMBER   MAY
FEBRUARY   NOVEMBER
JANUARY   OCTOBER
JULY   SEPTEMBER

PUZZLE 36: VEGETABLES

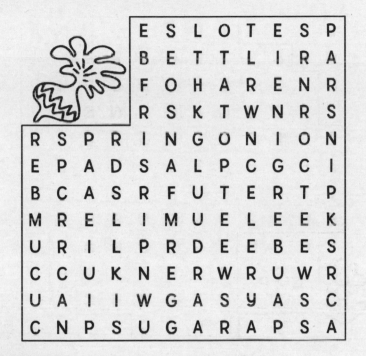

```
          E  S  L  O  T  E  S  P
          B  E  T  T  L  I  R  A
          F  O  H  A  R  E  N  R
          R  S  K  T  W  N  R  S
    R  S  P  R  I  N  G  O  N  I  O  N
    E  P  A  D  S  A  L  P  C  G  C  I
    B  C  A  S  R  F  U  T  E  R  T  P
    M  R  E  L  I  M  U  E  L  E  E  K
    U  R  I  L  P  R  D  E  E  B  E  S
    C  C  U  K  N  E  R  W  R  U  W  R
    U  A  I  I  W  G  A  S  Y  A  S  C
    C  N  P  S  U  G  A  R  A  P  S  A
```

ASPARAGUS	PARSNIP
AUBERGINE	PEA
CARROT	PUMPKIN
CAULIFLOWER	RADISH
CELERY	SPRING ONION
CRESS	SWEDE
CUCUMBER	SWEETCORN
GARLIC	SWEET POTATO
KALE	TURNIP
LEEK	

PUZZLE 37: FOOTBALL

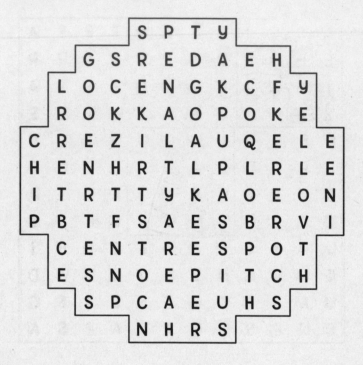

```
            S P T Y
          G S R E D A E H
        L O C E N G K C F Y
        R O K K A O P O K E
    C R E Z I L A U Q E L E
    H E N H R T L P L R L E
    I T R T T Y K A O E O N
    P B T F S A E S B R V I
      C E N T R E S P O T
      E S N O E P I T C H
        S P C A E U H S
            N H R S
```

BALL	KIT
BENCH	PASS
CENTRE SPOT	PENALTY AREA
CHIP	PITCH
CROSS	SCORE
EQUALIZER	STRIKER
FOUL	TACKLE
GOALKEEPER	VOLLEY
HEADER	

PUZZLE 38: MAGICIANS

A	S	S	I	S	T	A	N	T	A	H	A
E	P	O	R	D	E	R	I	A	P	E	R
T	N	O	I	T	C	I	D	E	R	P	A
S	A	W	I	N	H	A	L	F	B	O	E
I	I	T	E				Y	L	R	P
T	C	C	G				R	U	D	P
D	I	O	D				O	B	E	A
D	G	B	I				M	T	T	S
L	A	I	B	N	C	A	P	E	H	T	I
E	M	T	S	A	S	I	T	M	G	O	D
B	M	I	N	D	R	E	A	D	I	N	G
M	A	G	I	C	W	A	N	D	L	K	N

ASSISTANT   MAGICIAN
CAPE   MAGIC WAND
COINS   MEMORY FEAT
DICE   MIND-READING
DISAPPEAR   PREDICTION
HAT   RABBIT
KNOTTED ROPE   REPAIRED ROPE
LIGHT BULB   SAW IN HALF

PUZZLE 39: MONKEYS

```
O  S  A  K  I  H  Y  G  R  R  Z  A
D  C  Q  A  O  O  Y  A  D  N  L  E
E  G  L  U  D  N  T  E  S  U  I  B
S  H  U  C  I  A  B  A  N  H  L  S
O  A  E  G  M  R  O  L  O  W  A  Y
N  W  H  A  A  L  R  W  G  T  N  M
B  T  R  Z  N  E  L  E  A  R  G  H
U  I  Z  H  D  E  R  P  L  Q  U  H
N  A  R  I  R  P  O  R  R  G  R  N
S  N  P  N  I  H  C  U  P  A  C  R
I  S  C  O  L  O  B  U  S  A  U  O
A  D  E  T  L  I  A  B  K  L  O  A
```

CAPUCHIN	PATAS
COLOBUS	ROLOWAY
DEBRAZZAS	SAKI
HOWLER	SNUB-NOSED
LANGUR	SPIDER
MANDRILL	SQUIRREL
NIGHT	TAMARIN

PUZZLE 40: SHARKS

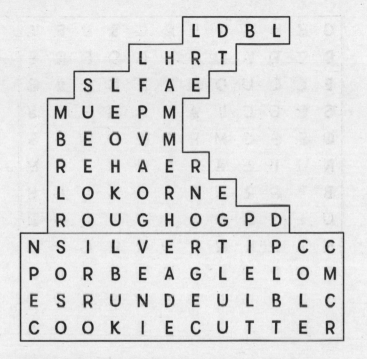

```
                    L D B L
                  L H R T
                S L F A E
              M U E P M
              B E O V M
              R E H A E R
              R L O K O R N E
              R O U G H O G P D
N S I L V E R T I P C C
P O R B E A G L E L O M
E S R U N D E U L B L C
C O O K I E C U T T E R
```

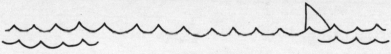

BLUE	MAKO
BULL	NURSE
COOKIECUTTER	PORBEAGLE
COPPER	REEF
HAMMERHEAD	ROUGH
HORN	SEVENGILL
LEOPARD	SILVERTIP

PUZZLE 41: LAUGHING

```
N H K M A E R C S L F K
R R T E E H E E C E R E
O E E L C A C K L E L C
K B E L L Y L A U G H W
A E G U F F A W S H E S
R U I E M A E N A L N E
C T G R A R I H K I L L
A I G K H C A C G T A E
H T L K K S U G R E H L
O T E E A H E O P E A R
O E R H C R H H H R E T
T R O A R C O S K E L B
```

BELLY-LAUGH	LARK
CACKLE	PEAL
CHORTLE	ROAR
CHUCKLE	SCREAM
GIGGLE	SHRIEK
GUFFAW	SNICKER
HA HA	SNIGGER
HE HE	TEE-HEE
HOOT	TITTER

PUZZLE 42: TROPICAL BIRDS

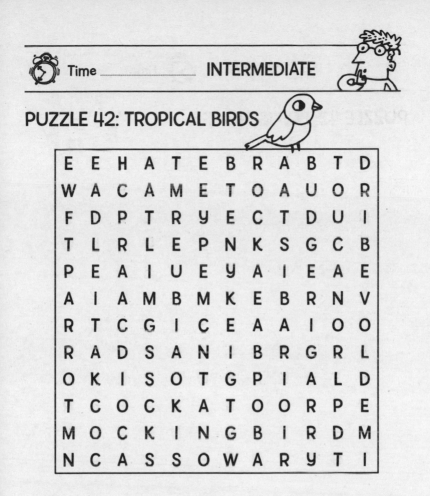

E	E	H	A	T	E	B	R	A	B	T	D
W	A	C	A	M	E	T	O	A	U	O	R
F	D	P	T	R	Y	E	C	T	D	U	I
T	L	R	L	E	P	N	K	S	G	C	B
P	E	A	I	U	E	Y	A	I	E	A	E
A	I	A	M	B	M	K	E	B	R	N	V
R	T	C	G	I	C	E	A	A	I	O	O
R	A	D	S	A	N	I	B	R	G	R	L
O	K	I	S	O	T	G	P	I	A	L	D
T	C	O	C	K	A	T	O	O	R	P	E
M	O	C	K	I	N	G	B	I	R	D	M
N	C	A	S	S	O	W	A	R	Y	T	I

ANI
BARBET
BUDGERIGAR
CASSOWARY
COCKATIEL
COCKATOO
FLAMINGO
HARPY EAGLE
LORIKEET

LOVEBIRD
MACAW
MOCKINGBIRD
MYNA BIRD
PARAKEET
PARROT
PLUME BIRD
TOUCAN
TROPICBIRD

PUZZLE 43: BRITISH KINGS

```
W  E  R  I  C  H  A  R  D  R  M  G
N  D  L  A  B  L  E  H  T  E  A  F
A  D  N  U  G  D  T  C  L  E  I  F
Y  E  A  T  H  D  H  A  R  O  L  D
J  R  T  Y  R  A  E  M  D  U  L  E
A  F  S  H  R  E  L  S  W  D  I  L
M  L  L  L  E  N  B  L  J  A  W  F
E  A  E  N  T  L  E  G  R  O  E  G
S  S  H  F  A  H  R  H  E  R  H  L
F  L  T  L  T  S  T  E  P  H  E  N
E  T  E  E  D  M  U  N  D  T  H  F
T  C  A  N  U  T  E  D  W  A  R  D
```

AETHELBALD	EDWARD
AETHELBERT	EGBERT
AETHELRED	GEORGE
AETHELSTAN	HAROLD
AETHELWULF	HENRY
ALFRED	JAMES
CANUTE	JOHN
CHARLES	RICHARD
EDGAR	STEPHEN
EDMUND	WILLIAM

PUZZLE 44: THINGS THAT FLY

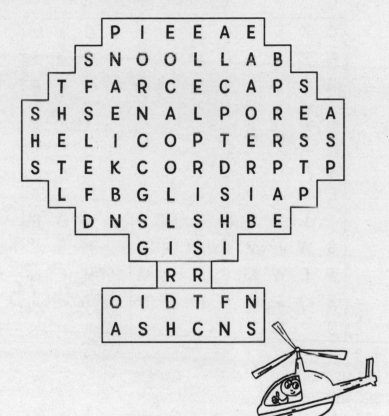

```
          P  I  E  E  A  E
       S  N  O  O  L  L  A  B
    T  F  A  R  C  E  C  A  P  S
 S  H  S  E  N  A  L  P  O  R  E  A
 H  E  L  I  C  O  P  T  E  R  S  S
 S  T  E  K  C  O  R  D  R  P  T  P
    L  F  B  G  L  I  S  I  A  P
       D  N  S  L  S  H  B  E
          G  I  S  I
             R  R
       O  I  D  T  F  N
       A  S  H  C  N  S
```

AEROPLANES   FRISBEES
AIRSHIPS   GLIDERS
BALLOONS   HELICOPTERS
BATS   ROCKETS
BIRDS   SPACECRAFT

PUZZLE 45: AREAS OF WATER

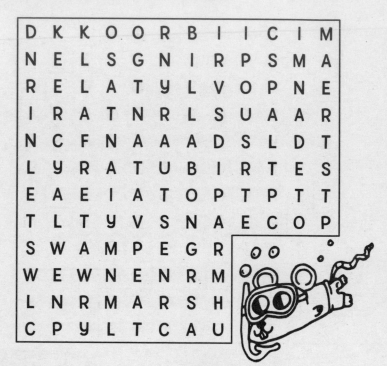

```
D  K  K  O  O  R  B  I  I  C  I  M
N  E  L  S  G  N  I  R  P  S  M  A
R  E  L  A  T  Y  L  V  O  P  N  E
I  R  A  T  N  R  L  S  U  A  A  R
N  C  F  N  A  A  A  D  S  L  D  T
L  Y  R  A  T  U  B  I  R  T  E  S
E  A  E  I  A  T  O  P  T  P  T  T
T  L  T  Y  V  S  N  A  E  C  O  P
S  W  A  M  P  E  G  R
W  E  W  N  E  N  R  M
L  N  R  M  A  R  S  H
C  P  Y  L  T  C  A  U
```

BILLABONG	RAPIDS
BROADS	RIVER
BROOK	RIVULET
CANAL	SPRING
CREEK	STRAIT
DELTA	STREAM
ESTUARY	SWAMP
INLET	TARN
MARSH	TRIBUTARY
OCEAN	WATERFALL

PUZZLE 46: VAMPIRES

```
E  E  H  G  A  R  L  I  C  Y  E  T
I  K  O  B  E  R  T  Y  K  K  C  I
V  B  L  O  O  D  E  O  A  S  H  C
B  B  Y  E  K  R  O  T  Y  R  T  I
H  L  W  C  D  P  S  L  S  L  E  M
T  R  A  N  S  Y  L  V  A  N  I  A
M  I  T  C  I  V  S  T  T  D  O  I
S  I  E  E  K  F  R  H  N  Y  T  M
S  I  R  E  E  O  F  I  A  E  K  C
O  E  P  R  M  T  G  O  F  D  C  S
R  A  O  M  O  H  H  E  C  M  O  K
C  H  I  T  T  R  E  V  L  I  S  W
```

BLACK	MIRROR
BLOOD	MONSTER
CAPE	NECK
COFFIN	SHADOW
CROSS	SILVER
FANTASY	SPOOKY
GARLIC	STAKE
HOLY WATER	TEETH
IMMORTAL	TRANSYLVANIA
MIDNIGHT	VICTIM

PUZZLE 47: FIREWORKS

```
T A W H I S T L E R A B
E E R Y E P H I H C A E
L X E A R A S F F R T B
D P K L I R I I R U U W
N L C P F K F A H T B F
A O A S N L G C T O O S
C S R I O E A E U U R P
N I C D B R R Q N A E I
A O E I A F U T T B S N
M N R P L E A R U E I N
O C I Y T I O T C A K E
R O F A N M H S A L F R
```

BARRAGE

BONFIRE

BOUQUET

BUTTERFLY

CAKE

DISPLAY

EXPLOSION

FIRECRACKER

FISH

FLASH

FOUNTAIN

MORTAR

PARACHUTE

ROMAN CANDLE

SPARKLER

SPINNER

TUBE

WHISTLER

PUZZLE 48: WINDS

```
R E G J T O R N A D O Y
L R N Y E S E U R E A L
D Y I D L T T G C O E R
N H L R N R S N D E A E
I P I R A I E T G I E T
W E A R E L W H R O N S
E Z V S U H H S T E D A
D T E B G P T S S R A E
A B R E G R U U A O O M
R U P A E G O W O U R N
T E L A R T S I M S U C
S E M L I V E D T S U D
```

AIRSTREAM	NORTHERLY
CROSSWIND	PREVAILING
DUST DEVIL	SOUTHERLY
EASTERLY	SOUTHWESTER
GALE	TORNADO
GUST	TRADE WIND
JET STREAM	TURBULENCE
MISTRAL	ZEPHYR

PUZZLE 49: SNAKES

```
R R O T C I R T S N O C
S · D E A T H A D D E R
K R A I T       C R R P
M A M B A       N E S L
                I A R B
V H T U O M N O T T O C
I R I B B O N S N A K E
P R A T T L E S N A K E
E A P
R I N G H A L S
S I H P O R D N E D
B C A R P E T S N A K E
```

ASP	KRAIT
BOA	MAMBA
CARPET SNAKE	RACER
CONSTRICTOR	RATTLESNAKE
COTTONMOUTH	RIBBON SNAKE
DEATH ADDER	RINGHALS
DENDROPHIS	VIPER

PUZZLE 50: SPORTS

```
Y E K C O H E C I G R I
R L U O L A C R O S S E
B U L G L L A B T O O F
B I G A A O A N C Y C T
T O N B B E P B E A C E
T N B A Y T L R T A E N
E N G S E U E Y E F R N
K O N E L R N K B T O I
C I I B L E E I S G A S
I L W A O L I L O A U W
R C O L V N E G A N B R
C U R L I N G I H Y L I
```

BASEBALL	ROWING
BASKETBALL	RUGBY LEAGUE
BOBSLEIGH	RUGBY UNION
CRICKET	SOCCER
CURLING	SOFTBALL
FOOTBALL	TENNIS
ICE HOCKEY	VOLLEYBALL
LACROSSE	WATER POLO
RELAY	

PUZZLE 51: SUPER POWERS

```
G N T N I Y T V L Y N N
N Y T O T T Y O O T O N
I T E N E I T L R I I O
L Y L O L L I I T L S I
A H E I E A V C N I I S
E T K T P T E T O B V I
H A I A O R G H C I T V
L P N T R O N G D S A T
V E E U T M O I N I E H
G L S M I M L L I V H G
O E I M N I S F M N L I
R T S E G G V K T I E N
```

FLIGHT

HEALING

HEAT VISION

IMMORTALITY

INVISIBILITY

LONGEVITY

MIND CONTROL

MUTATION

NIGHT VISION

RESURRECTION

TELEKINESIS

TELEPATHY

TELEPORTING

PUZZLE 52: WEREWOLVES

```
U E I N       B R R H
E A T H   C   F E E B
E H N A       U T T E
O T C I       R F N A
F H L R M M S A U I U S
R G A Y U A N L P H H T
I I W T M S L U B S L I
G L A O I M L E G E N D
H N W T O E E T D P O T
T O I O G D P I N A M U
E O N N H T S B O H E D
N M H T G N E R T S D G
```

ANIMAL   HUNTER
BEAST   LEGEND
BITE   LUPINE
CLAW   MOONLIGHT
DEMON   MUTANT
FRIGHTEN   SHAPE-SHIFTER
FULL MOON   SPELL
FUR   STRENGTH
HAIRY   TRANSITION
HOWL   WOODS

PUZZLE 53: MUSIC GENRES

S	U	C	G	C	D	G	I		
B	L	A	K	O	I	G	N		
R	N	L	K	U	S	A	D		
E	O	Y	N	N	C	P	I		
F	I	P	G	T	O	L	E	J	A	Z	Z
A	S	S	A	R	G	E	U	L	B	I	F
E	U	O	M	Y	U	N	C	O	N	F	N
S	F	P	B	B	G	N	N	S	G	Y
U	P	E	I	L	F	H	G	E	A	G	O
O	P	R	E	U	C	Y	U	E	O	R	A
H	F	A	N	E	A	G	G	E	R	O	T
T	A	K	T	S	N	A	L	E	S	T	O

AMBIENT
BLUEGRASS
BLUES
CALYPSO
COUNTRY
DISCO
FOLK
FUNK
FUSION
GOSPEL

GRUNGE
HOUSE
INDIE
JAZZ
JUNGLE
OPERA
REGGAE
SOUL
TECHNO
TRANCE

PUZZLE 54: SHELLS

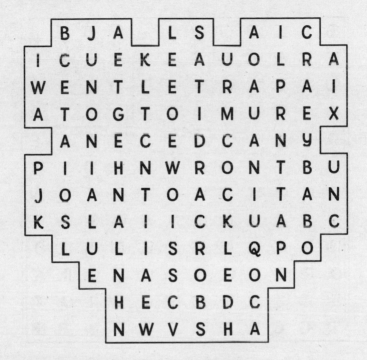

```
B J A   L S   A I C
I C U E K E A U O L R A
W E N T L E T R A P A I
A T O G T O I M U R E X
  A N E C E D C A N Y
P I I H N W R O N T B U
J O A N T O A C I T A N
K S L A I I C K U A B C
  L U L I S R L Q P O
    E N A S O E O N
    H E C B D C
    N W V S H A
```

BABY EAR	DOSINIA
BUTTERCUP	JINGLES
CARDITA	JUNONIA
CERITH	MUREX
CLAM	NATICA
COCKLE	SCALLOP
CONCH	VENUS
CONE	WENTLETRAP
COQUINA	WHELK

PUZZLE 55: CAKES

```
B C C S Y R I A F B T B
T C H C U P C A K E R D
U S E R E E F F O C A G
B P E K I A P P L E T R
I I S R L S M A R B L E
R E E I O A T B F G L B
T C C K D F R M N T E N
H C A A A E K I A G W E
D L K R G C D C N S E T
A E E N R D A O A B K T
Y S I P E O P E W L A A
R G C W C S T R T N B B
```

APPLE
BAKEWELL TART
BATTENBERG
BIRTHDAY
BLACK FOREST
CARROT
CHEESECAKE
CHRISTMAS
COFFEE

CUPCAKE
ECCLES
FAIRY
GINGERBREAD
MARBLE
SPONGE
TEACAKE
UPSIDE-DOWN
WEDDING

PUZZLE 56: REPTILES

```
T C H A M E L E O N B M
H R E N O I K S O O S R
O T L O Z A K C X E A O
R O T A N I A T A L N W
N A R S N I U T L C A W
Y D U K M R U I X E U O
D N T A T R G S R I G L
E G N L T A W M R A I S
V E E L T R U T D N O P
I C E O T O R T O I S E
L K R E L I D O C O R C
N O G A R D O D O M O K
```

ALLIGATOR	LIZARD
BOX TURTLE	POND TURTLE
CAIMAN	SEA TURTLE
CHAMELEON	SKINK
CROCODILE	SLOWWORM
GECKO	SNAKE
GREEN TURTLE	THORNY DEVIL
IGUANA	TORTOISE
KOMODO DRAGON	

PUZZLE 57: WAYS TO MOVE

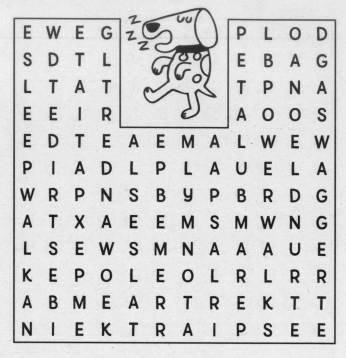

```
E W E G       P L O D
S D T L       E B A G
L T A T       T P N A
E E I R       A O O S
E D T E A E M A L W E W
P I A D L P L A U E L A
W R P N S B Y P B R D G
A T X A E E M S M W N G
L S E W S M N A A A U E
K E P O L E O L R L R R
A B M E A R T R E K T T
N I E K T R A I P S E E
```

BESTRIDE

LOPE

MOSEY ALONG

PAD

PARADE

PLOD

POWER-WALK

PROMENADE

RAMBLE

ROAM

SLEEPWALK

SNEAK

SWAGGER

TRAIPSE

TRAMPLE

TREK

TRUNDLE

WANDER

PUZZLE 58: PONY BREEDS

```
A  S  L  E  C  A  B  A  L  I  G  F
I  N  I  O  A  O  L  M  T  A  R  R
H  L  Y  N  O  P  H  S  L  E  W  D
H  F  E  L  L  U  E  I  N  C  N  A
I  A  D  D  C  R  C  C  O  A  F  L
G  L  N  U  O  I  H  N  L  U  A  E
H  A  L  F  A  S  N  T  D  C  R  S
L  B  W  N  A  E  E  X  M  O  O  R
A  E  N  D  M  H  A  C  K  N  E  Y
N  L  D  A  S  T  U  R  I  A  N  A
D  L  R  O  O  M  T  R  A  D  L  A
E  A  M  C  S  A  O  T  U  S  A  B
```

ASTURIAN	FELL
BALI	FRENCH SADDLE
BASUTO	GALICIAN
CONNEMARA	HACKNEY
DALES	HIGHLAND
DARTMOOR	HUCUL
DELI	NEW FOREST
EXMOOR	SHETLAND
FAROE	WELSH PONY

PUZZLE 59: DOG BREEDS

```
E H D N U H S H C A D Z
J N G R E Y H O U N D C
G A A S A F G H A N O P
O P C D C Z C I X L O I
D O S K T H T D L D P N
P O M E R A N I A N O S
E D A E M U E A P E I C
E L C L O L S R U S N H
H E A H J T R S G Z T E
S D X R E T R I E V E R
L O R O D A R B A L R R
F C H I H U A H U A L C
```

AFGHAN
CHIHUAHUA
COLLIE
DACHSHUND
DALMATIAN
FOXHOUND
GREAT DANE
GREYHOUND
JACK RUSSELL
LABRADOR

PINSCHER
POINTER
POMERANIAN
POODLE
PUG
RETRIEVER
SCHNAUZER
SHEEPDOG
SPITZ

PUZZLE 60: CAT BREEDS

```
Y T A A N A I R E B I S
G U A M N A I T P Y G E
O B X R W X B E N G A L
X X O E O I N I J P M U
E E X M R K X A E T A Z
R R N E B H V R M O I A
N N Y F A A S T N Y N S
O A H P N I Y I I G E O
G M P E A C B E N E C J
E R S N V M B T A R O O
R E D N A L H G I H O I
O G I B H F L E W D N C
```

BAMBINO

BENGAL

BOMBAY

CORNISH REX

DWELF

EGYPTIAN MAU

GERMAN REX

HAVANA BROWN

HIGHLANDER

JAVANESE

KORAT

MAINE COON

MANX

OJOS AZULES

OREGON REX

PERSIAN

SIBERIAN

SPHYNX

TOYGER

PUZZLE 61: PETS

```
A  R  N  G  U  P  N  T
N  L  S  E  U  R  O  F
A  P  L  P  K  R  E  P
U  G  P  I  T  C  G  T
G  Y  U  O  H  S  I  F  D  L  O  G
I  E  I  I  N  C  P  H  P  A  O  R
D  S  G  S  N  Y  N  A  C  D  D  E
E  B  U  D  G  E  R  I  G  A  R  T
T  E  E  K  A  R  A  P  H  N  A  S
S  H  C  E  O  C  C  P  A  C  Z  M
U  U  A  T  N  E  T  T  I  K  I  A
D  R  A  B  B  I  T  A  O  G  L  H
```

BUDGERIGAR	IGUANA
CAT	KITTEN
CHICKEN	LIZARD
CHINCHILLA	PARAKEET
DOG	PARROT
DUCK	PIGEON
GOAT	PONY
GOLDFISH	PUPPY
GUINEA PIG	RABBIT
HAMSTER	TORTOISE

PUZZLE 62: CLOTHES

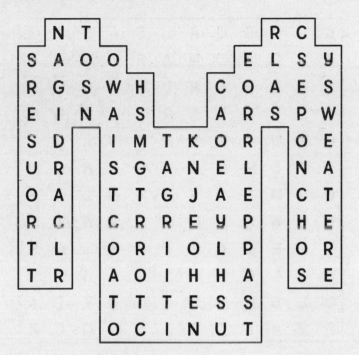

```
  N T                    R C
S A O O            E L S Y
R G S W H      C O A E S
E I N A S      A R S P W
S D   I M T K O R   O E
U R   S G A N E L   N A
O A   T T G J A E   C T
R C   C R R E Y P   H E
T L   O R I O L P   O R
T R   A O I H H A   S E
      T T T E S S
      O C I N U T
```

CARDIGAN
CLOAK
JERSEY
LEGGINGS
PANTS
PONCHO
PYJAMAS

SARONG
SHORTS
SWEATER
TROUSERS
T-SHIRT
TUNIC
WAISTCOAT

PUZZLE 63: MAGIC

```
C R Y S T A L B A L L G
T N E M T N A H C N E Y
R W D S W F L T D O E R
W I T C H A R T I C H I
O Z V L M A N L V A G T
P A L M R E A D I N G U
O R M R P T H M N L A A
G D A R U O S C A N T L
Y I N C A N T A T I O N
H C I G A H H I I A A R
L L E P S O C O O T D A
R E R E C R O S N N P A
```

CHARM
CRYSTAL BALL
DIVINATION
ENCHANTMENT
INCANTATION
PALM READING
POTION

RITUAL
SORCERER
SPELL
TOAD
WAND
WITCH
WIZARD

PUZZLE 64: ART SUPPLIES

```
F  F  D  L  A  C  R  Y  L  I  C  K
E  R  N  N  G  L  U  E  R  A  N  P
C  G  P  L  R  N  O  B  B  I  R  B
F  F  N  E  F  E  L  T  T  I  P  C
L  P  X  O  R  N  O  B  M  I  L  H
C  I  I  I  P  C  C  E  G  A  R  A
F  N  C  L  A  S  R  M  Y  R  A  L
B  O  U  N  L  L  E  T  S  A  P  K
R  Y  V  C  E  N  T  T
U  A  M  E  T  P  A  I
S  R  C  Y  T  G  W  T
H  C  D  A  E  R  H  T
```

ACRYLIC	OIL
BRUSH	PALETTE
CANVAS	PASTEL
CHALK	PENCIL
CLAY	PIGMENT
CRAYON	PRIMER
FELT TIP	RIBBON
FIXER	SPONGE
GLUE	THREAD
INK	WATERCOLOUR

ADVANCED

PUZZLE 65: UNDER THE SEA

```
Q H E S R O H A E S F R F
B R S E H D D E L A E S W
D O L P H I N I C T E E E
D H A R B U P N A T R A L
R C E R S Q H W N M G W A
A N L O B S T E R L R E H
E A T N I L R T A E U E W
L E R F A R S T B R C D M
D E U S U P O T C O N K A
N B T C O U A H R
W F D N W L I A A
H O G E R N L E B
R E T S Y O T H R
```

ALGAE	LOBSTER	SEAWEED
ANCHOR	MERMAID	SHIPWRECK
BARNACLE	OCTOPUS	SPONGE
CORAL	OYSTER	SQUID
CRAB	REEF	TURTLE
CURRENT	SALT WATER	URCHIN
DOLPHIN	SEAHORSE	WHALE
FISH	SEAL	

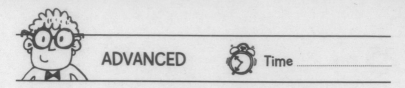

PUZZLE 66: WILD WEST

```
H G W C O W B O Y T O R B
L A S S O W R A N G L E R
A B E A T T E D N E V H A
O E L N M D G R N N A T E
R L J A I L N N O O L A S
E D W H C M I D O T H E B
G D W A R K L P N S F L A
G A E G L A S Y H B F O N
R S T P N T N M G M I T D
      M A U C I O R S I
      R A G O H T E I T
      R E T S L O H P L
      H O R S E I S G G
```

BANDIT	JAIL	SADDLEBAG
BLACKSMITH	LASSO	SALOON
COWBOY	LEATHER	SHERIFF
GANG	MINE	STAMPEDE
GUNSLINGER	OUTLAW	TOMBSTONE
HIGH NOON	PISTOL	VENDETTA
HOLSTER	RANCH	WRANGLER
HORSE	RAWHIDE	

PUZZLE 67: FAIRY-TALE CHARACTERS

R	B	M	U	H	T	M	O	T	E	W	O	R
D	E	D	A	O	B	M	T	T	I	I	U	U
S	R	D	D	T	J	A	E	C	H	G	D	C
R	P	A	R	E	T	A	K	C	L	B	S	I
A	E	I	P	I	S	E	C	Y	L	I	K	N
E	P	T	C	U	D	O	S	K	E	G	C	D
B	R	L	S	W	N	I	E	I	S	B	O	E
E	I	S	I	I	S	Z	N	I	N	A	L	R
E	N	T	P	T	S	F	E	G	A	D	I	E
R	C	T	E	A	Y	P	W	L	H	W	D	L
H	E	R	T	L	E	T	E	R	G	O	L	L
T	S	N	O	W	W	H	I	T	E	L	O	A
T	S	L	R	G	E	N	A	R	S	F	G	D

BIG BAD WOLF
CINDERELLA
GOLDILOCKS
GRETEL
HANSEL
JACK
PINOCCHIO
PRINCESS
RAPUNZEL
RED RIDING HOOD

SNOW WHITE
STEPSISTER
THREE BEARS
TOM THUMB
UGLY SISTERS
WICKED WITCH

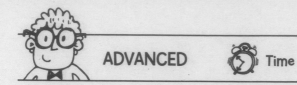
PUZZLE 68: MOUNTAINS

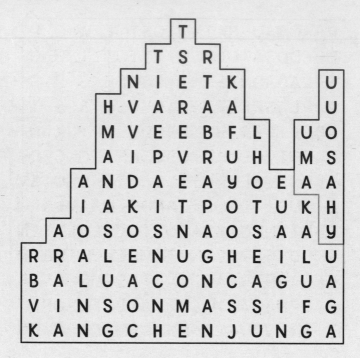

ACONCAGUA	MANASLU
BROAD PEAK	MOUNT EVEREST
CHO OYU	NANGA PARBAT
KANGCHENJUNGA	RAINIER
LHOTSE	VINSON MASSIF
MAKALU	

PUZZLE 69: BONES

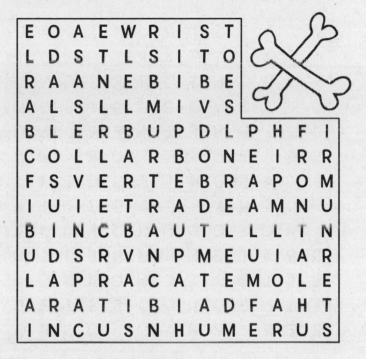

```
E O A E W R I S T
L D S T L S I T O
R A A N E B I B E
A L S L L M I V S
B L E R B U P D L P H F I
C O L L A R B O N E I R R
F S V E R T E B R A P O M
I U I E T R A D E A M N U
B I N C B A U T L L I N
U D S R V N P M E U I A R
L A P R A C A T E M O L E
A R A T I B I A D F A H T
I N C U S N H U M E R U S
```

COLLARBONE	MANDIBLE	SHOULDER BLADE
FEMUR	METACARPAL	STERNUM
FIBULA	METATARSAL	TEMPORAL
FRONTAL	PATELLA	TIBIA
HIP	PELVIS	TOES
HUMERUS	RADIUS	VERTEBRA
INCUS	RIBS	WRIST

PUZZLE 70: MYTHS AND LEGENDS

```
M T N T B T R U H T R A C
I E A L A C H I L L E S I
R O D O L G D R A G O N N
G I L U D O O H N I B O R
H D I E S I R A R R D W R
S L A T L A N T I S A M A
E K A L E H T F O Y D A L
M O T N A H P R S G I I Y
A M U E C A C U R F R D R
G S S T M E R M A I D E I
L T I R R A L E L O W N A
I W A E C T O O F G I B F
G E R I P M A V T S O H G
```

ACHILLES	LADY OF THE LAKE	TROLL
ARTHUR	LANCELOT	VAMPIRE
ATLANTIS	MEDUSA	WITCH
BIGFOOT	MERMAID	
DRAGON	OGRE	
FAIRY	PHANTOM	
GHOST	ROBIN HOOD	
GILGAMESH	SNOW MAIDEN	
ICARUS	SORCERER	

PUZZLE 71: PRECIOUS STONES

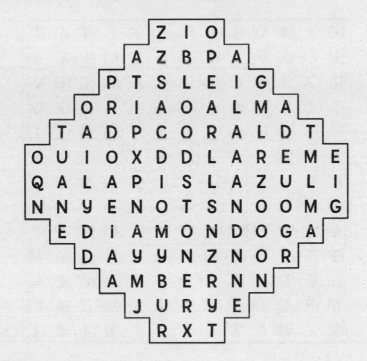

```
        Z I O
      A Z B P A
    P T S L E I G
  O R I A O A L M A
T A D P C O R A L D T
O U I O X D D L A R E M E
Q A L A P I S L A Z U L I
N N Y E N O T S N O O M G
  E D I A M O N D O G A
    D A Y Y N Z N O R
      A M B E R N N
        J U R Y E
          R X T
```

AGATE	MOONSTONE
AMBER	OBSIDIAN
BLOODSTONE	ONYX
CORAL	OPAL
DIAMOND	PEARL
EMERALD	QUARTZ
GARNET	RUBY
JADE	TOPAZ
LAPIS LAZULI	

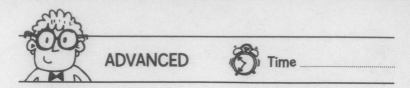
PUZZLE 72: US STATES

```
O L A W A S H I N G T O N
H D N A L S I E D O H R E
A A I N R O F I L A C O W
D D L O U I S I A N A K M
I I O Z         W O L E
R R R I         R A A X
U O A R         S W H I
O L C A         O O O C
S F H M         M I M O
S T T E S U H C A S S A M
I E R I H S P M A H W E N
M S O U T H D A K O T A I
P E N N S Y L V A N I A I
```

ARIZONA

CALIFORNIA

FLORIDA

HAWAII

IDAHO

IOWA

LOUISIANA

MASSACHUSETTS

MISSOURI

NEW HAMPSHIRE

NEW MEXICO

NORTH CAROLINA

OKLAHOMA

PENNSYLVANIA

RHODE ISLAND

SOUTH DAKOTA

WASHINGTON

PUZZLE 73: ARTISTS

```
D  T  I  A  O  L  L  E  T  A  N  O  D
E  S  N  L  T  S  R  I  H  E  I  M  V
K  P  I  S  A  N  O  T  O  L  E  T  A
O  I  L  G  Z  D  M  T  L  G  T  I  N
O  T  L  F  N  I  T  E  B  A  S  N  D
N  T  A  S  L  O  V  Z  E  N  N  T  E
I  E  V  K  I  A  R  N  I  I  E  O  R
N  M  A  G  I  A  K  E  N  E  T  R  A
G  O  C  H  D  H  Z  R  L  R  H  E  A
O  C  C  M  A  S  S  O  N  L  C  T  C
C  A  U  L  F  I  E  L  D  T  I  T  K
M  I  C  H  E  L  A  N  G  E  L  O  H
E  G  O  I  L  L  E  C  I  T  T  O  B
```

BOTTICELLI	HIRST	MICHELANGELO
CAULFIELD	HOLBEIN	PISANO
CAVALLINI	KALF	REINAGLE
DALI	KLIMT	SIGNORELLI
DE KOONING	LICHTENSTEIN	TINTORETTO
DONATELLO	LORENZETTI	VAN DER AACK
GIACOMETTI	MACHIAVELLI	ZAIS
GIOTTO	MASSON	

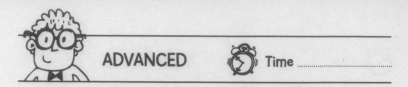
PUZZLE 74: OLYMPIC SPORTS

```
              N O T N I M D A B
              T L C S N G W C O
              H Y W O Y N R L I
              C I L M E I E L T
G S L L M H N E K V S A A
G N I M T A B I C I T B E
G N I A S C W U O D L T K
G N I T F I L T H G I E W
G R I E O T N O D I N K O
T C I W O O T N L D G S N
S J U D O N H B E O C A D
Y R E H C R A S I T E B O
J U M P I N G C F K O T H
```

ARCHERY
BADMINTON
BASKETBALL
CANOEING
CYCLING
DIVING
FIELD HOCKEY
GYMNASTICS
JUDO

ROWING
SHOOTING
SWIMMING
TAE KWON DO
TENNIS
TRIATHLON
WEIGHTLIFTING
WRESTLING

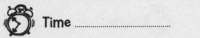
PUZZLE 75: CAPITAL CITIES

```
O N K L H E L S I N K I R
N K W U W S B B O N N C L
E O O O A M S T E R D A M
W K C E S L G G E R L N A
D G S S H N A D E U N B S
E N O A I H A L X M A E L
L A M L N R O E U B O R E
H B L E G T M V A M C R S
I E P L T B I S O O P A S
W O E A O E I A L Y B U U
C B W U N D B S G O K B R
A A R N D N O D N O L O B
G G A A C B U D A P E S T
```

ADDIS ABABA   KUALA LUMPUR   TOKYO
AMSTERDAM   LONDON   VIENNA
BANGKOK   LUXEMBOURG   WASHINGTON DC
BELGRADE   MOSCOW   WELLINGTON
BERN   NEW DELHI
BRUSSELS   OSLO
BUDAPEST   OTTAWA
CANBERRA   ROME
COPENHAGEN   SANTIAGO
HELSINKI   SEOUL

PUZZLE 76: SINGING

```
H T N A H C S T Y D C O O
Q N T O S E R E N A D E O
C U E E U N I R I O H C H
L S A L U C L N L N E E C
H Q U V T O R P T N C E W
S R L E E S P O E O S L L
M U H N O R I L O U N H P
L A R I I D B H R N P E Y
T V O H U R H O W U E T Q
R A C E A S H O D P I P E
I I T W Y C O H N U I O O
L T U O O R N L R W H O S
L H L Y O D E L O U H T L
```

CHANT
CHIRP
CHOIR
CHORUS
CROON
DUET
HUM
INTONE

PIPE
QUAVER
SERENADE
SOLO
TRILL
WARBLE
WHISTLE
YODEL

PUZZLE 77: NURSERY RHYMES

```
S R O C K A B Y E B A B Y
B N N B J A C K S P R A T
O E U T L D E L R I P T G
E U L B Y O B E L T T I L
T O E C S B A S P A I N B
C N O M I S E L P M I S E
L L E B G N O D G N I D D
I R E T S O F R O T C O D
M O L D K I N G C O L E E
Y P E E P O B E L T T I L
E I G R O P E I G R O E G
U P E T E R P I P E R H R
M O N D A Y S C H I L D L
```

DING DONG BELL
DOCTOR FOSTER
GEORGIE PORGIE
HOT CROSS BUNS
JACK SPRAT
LITTLE BO PEEP
LITTLE BOY BLUE
MONDAY'S CHILD
OLD KING COLE

PETER PIPER
ROCK A BYE BABY
SIMPLE SIMON

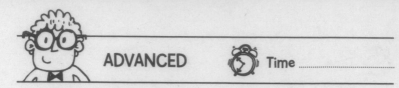
PUZZLE 78: CURRENCIES

```
A O O M I F Y O R U E R F
R A H U A H R T N F L R U
I F M A K R A N O K U F R
L O W H E C D O L L A R A
P R O T C N F R O O Z R D
D I N A R A O R O E T N F
A N Y N S N R R A O D L D
N T T I O E R D K N O T C
U K R B U Y Y A U R C E D
K Y N P E S O O I A S B M
O A O O T T P N N Y U A N
R T O D U C S E T U G H C
W G R E D L I U G I R T D
```

BAHT	FLORIN	LIRA
DINAR	FORINT	PESO
DOLLAR	FRANC	POUND
DRACHMA	GUILDER	WON
DRAM	KRONE	YEN
ESCUDO	KUNA	YUAN
EURO	KYAT	ZLOTY

PUZZLE 79: SPORTS CARS

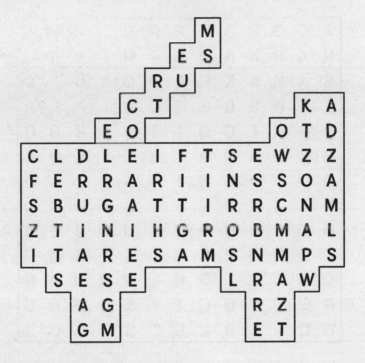

BMW
BUGATTI
FERRARI
KOENIGSEGG
LAMBORGHINI
LOTUS
MASERATI
MAZDA

MERCEDES
PANOZ
WESTFIELD

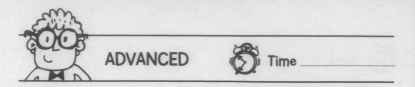
PUZZLE 80: CHINESE NEW YEAR ANIMALS

```
E  T  G  R  D  D  R  R  I
N  A  R  A  O  D  H  R  M
B  A  K  R  N  O  R  E  O
E  E  R  G  R  I  S  O  N
E  R  R  A  G  O  A  T  K  K  Y  G  O
N  S  T  A  I  Y  I  S  E  K  E  O  R
O  O  I  E  P  B  I  I  Y  R  X  A  O
R  X  G  K  B  R  H  S  B  T  K  D  N
G  O  E  A  D  O  G  A  O  O  Y  E  A
T  G  R  N  R  E  M  I  B  O  A  O  G
O  O  O  S  I  D  N  E  A  R  O  P  H
O  M  E  G  B  G  T  I  X  O  R  A  O
G  O  A  E  A  R  G  T  S  O  G  G  B
```

DOG	PIG
DRAGON	RABBIT
GOAT	RAT
HORSE	ROOSTER
MONKEY	SNAKE
OXEN	TIGER

PUZZLE 81: DANCES

```
O A P E T S K C I U Q R I
E A R I L O S P Y L A C I
K L N G U B R E T T I J A
L L L O N O O T L A O A N
A E A O T A O D X P S B E
W T M W R S H L O O O M R
E N S E H D E B A S F U A
K A D I R T N L S G A R C
A R I G R E E A R A O P A
C A S O C R N B K A M O M
X T C O T O O G M C H B B
A A O B V I A M U A O C A
O G N A D N A F C E L R R
```

BHANGRA   DISCO   MORRIS

BOOGALOO   FANDANGO   PASO DOBLE

BOOGIE-WOOGIE   FOXTROT   QUICKSTEP

BOSSA NOVA   JITTERBUG   ROCK AND ROLL

CAKEWALK   LAMBETH WALK   RUMBA

CALYPSO   MACARENA   SAMBA

CHARLESTON   MERENGUE   TARANTELLA

PUZZLE 82: SPIDERS

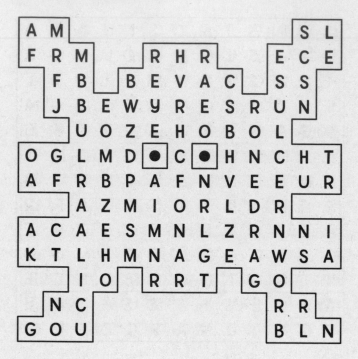

BROWN RECLUSE

CAMEL

CAVE

CELLAR

COMMON HOUSE

FISHING

GARDEN

HOBO

JUMPING

NURSERY WEB

REDBACK

TURRET

WOLF

ZEBRA

PUZZLE 83: ZODIAC SIGNS

A	H	N	S	T	R	O	S	N	E	M	S	A
E	I	L	S	L	E	R	C	O	A	A	U	A
F	E	I	S	E	I	F	M	I	B	P	P	L
L	I	S	A	O	R	T	D	P	C	E	R	A
W	A	T	E	R	B	E	A	R	E	R	M	C
B	I	M	I	L	N	S	H	O	U	S	A	I
E	I	O	L	L	A	R	L	C	G	N	S	B
L	T	U	C	S	H	C	S	S	R	A	M	R
L	B	F	R	C	B	T	S	C	F	A	E	T
L	A	T	E	A	N	W	O	T	W	I	N	S
A	O	A	N	N	I	S	U	B	A	O	S	E
B	T	B	F	L	P	R	S	S	I	I	B	H
C	A	E	A	E	W	S	W	L	A	F	L	O

ARCHER	RAM
BULL	SCALES
CRAB	SCORPION
FISH	SEA-GOAT
LION	TWINS
MAIDEN	WATER BEARER

PUZZLE 84: FAMOUS EXPLORERS

```
C U O B A L B O A K O O C
L E N O S E N N E I F A H
L S C U N R A M A G A D G
N I H G S V E S P U C C I
E E V A A Z O D N E M Z E
K S S I C U A M N R A A L
A E U N N K A T E I E I A
R M B V A G L E A K L D R
D O M I E N S E T S R F M
U G U L I E O T T S M U S
H I L L A R Y I O O U A B
G A O E B A F F I N N O N
N E C T A M U N D S E N C
```

AMUNDSEN	DRAKE	RALEIGH
BAFFIN	ERIKSSON	SHACKLETON
BALBOA	FIENNES	TASMAN
BOUGAINVILLE	FLINDERS	VESPUCCI
BURKE	GOMES	
COLUMBUS	HILLARY	
COOK	LIVINGSTONE	
COUSTEAU	MAGELLAN	
DA GAMA	MENDOZA	
DIAZ	NANSEN	

PUZZLE 85: 3D SHAPES

```
C E R P O L Y H E D R O N
C R T E T R A H E D R O N
C S T C R R U A T O R U S
I A O O Y R P O N D I C N
I D O E C L O Y E E C E M
M R T B C T I H R C O S H
S S N U U L A N O A P E T
O E A C B S R H D H M R N
L P N O O R C P E E E I N
E N M C I N D R O D R O D
H Y I I D E E I H R R P I
R R S U P Y C S C O O O C
H R E U N H R M H N P E N
```

CONE
CUBE
CUBOID
CYLINDER
DODECAHEDRON
ICOSAHEDRON
OCTAHEDRON
POLYHEDRON
PRISM

PYRAMID
SPHERE
TETRAHEDRON
TORUS

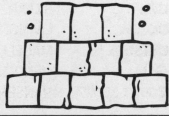

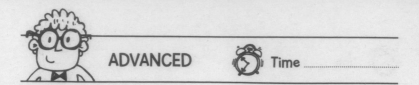
PUZZLE 86: PARTS OF A CASTLE

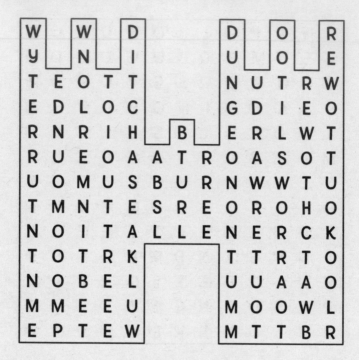

```
W     W     D           D     O     R
Y     N     I           U     O     R E
T E O T T           N U T R W
E D L O C           G D I E O
R N R I H     B     E R L W T
R U E O A A T R O A S O T
U O M U S B U R N W W T U
T M N T E S R E O R O H O
N O I T A L L E N E R C K
T O T R K           T T R T O
N O B E L           U U A A O
M M E E U           M O O W L
E P T E W           M T T B R
```

ARROW SLIT
BASTION
CRENELLATION
DITCH
DUNGEON
EMBRASURE
KEEP
LOOKOUT TOWER

MERLON
MOAT
MOTTE
MOUND
OUTER BAILEY
OUTER WARD
TURRET
WATCHTOWER

PUZZLE 87: ART STYLES

```
N N A I M E H O B T P K S
Q E U M E K C U V R R I U
M U O B S E S E I A E N P
S S A C D I N O B L R E R
I S I T L E B S L A A T E
L T R N T A T U O P I M
A A R I O R S C C T H C A
E R A A A Y O S Q P A A T
R N O C P C A C I E E R I
W C T K O O I R E C L T S
E X P R E S S I O N I S M
N O Z I B R A B O O T S O
V O R T I C I S M C E O M
```

ABSTRACT
ART DECO
BOHEMIAN
CONCEPTUAL ART
CUBISM
EXPRESSIONISM
KINETIC ART
NEOCLASSICISM

NEW REALISM
OP ART
PRE-RAPHAELITE
RAYONISM
ROCOCO
SUPREMATISM
VENETIAN
VORTICISM

PUZZLE 88: FRUIT JUICES

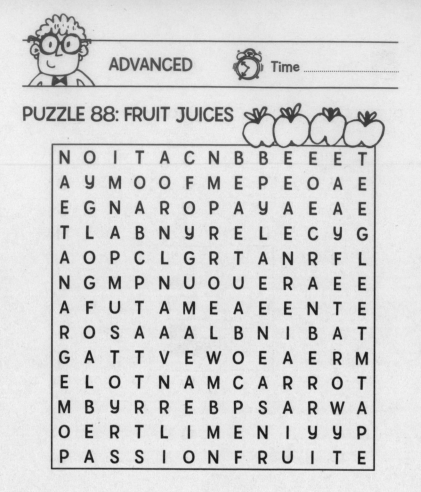

```
N O I T A C N B B E E T
A Y M O O F M E P E O A E
E G N A R O P A Y A E A E
T L A B N Y R E L E C Y G
A O P C L G R T A N R F L
N G M P N U O U E R A E E
A F U T A M E A E E N T E
R O S A A A L B N I B A T
G A T T V E W O E A E R M
E L O T N A M C A R R O T
M B Y R R E B P S A R W A
O E R T L I M E N I Y Y P
P A S S I O N F R U I T E
```

APPLE	LIME
BEETROOT	MANGO
BLUEBERRY	ORANGE
CARROT	PASSION FRUIT
CELERY	PEAR
CRANBERRY	POMEGRANATE
GRAPE	RASPBERRY
GUAVA	STRAWBERRY
LEMON	TOMATO

PUZZLE 89: PARTS OF A SHIP

```
M  R  E  D  N  E  F  S  A  L  O  O  N
L  U  L  I  G  A  N  G  W  A  Y  D  O
E  O  B  D  R  E  T  N  I  A  P  R  C
H  A  I  F  F  B  L  A  D  E  O  E  M
C  R  B  O              R  R  D  I
B  O  G  R              E  T  D  Z
W  L  U  E              K  H  U  Z
T  A  N  C              A  O  R  E
L  N  W  A              N  L  E  N
E  Y  A  S  C  R  O  W  S  N  E  S  T
E  A  L  T  G  N  I  G  G  I  R  B  L
H  R  E  L  L  E  P  O  R  P  B  I  J
W  D  B  E  A  M  A  I  N  S  A  I  L
```

BEAM	GANGWAY	PAINTER
BLADE	GUNWALE	PORTHOLE
BOW	HELM	PROPELLER
BRIDGE	HOLD	RIGGING
CABIN	JIB	RUDDER
CROW'S NEST	LANYARD	SALOON
FENDER	MAINSAIL	SPINNAKER
FORECASTLE	MIZZEN	WHEEL

PUZZLE 90: SHADES OF BLUE

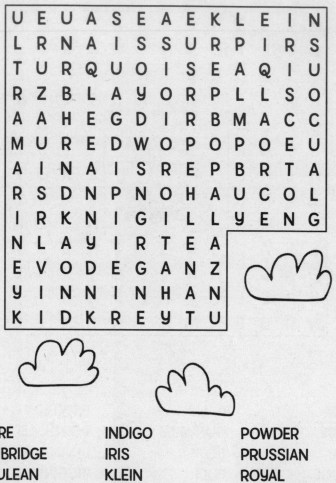

```
U E U A S E A E K L E I N
L R N A I S S U R P I R S
T U R Q U O I S E A Q I U
R Z B L A Y O R P L L S O
A A H E G D I R B M A C C
M U R E D W O P O P O E U
A I N A I S R E P B R T A
R S D N P N O H A U C O L
I R K N I G I L L Y E N G
N L A Y I R T E A
E V O D E G A N Z
Y I N N I N H A N
K I D K R E Y T U
```

AZURE	INDIGO	POWDER
CAMBRIDGE	IRIS	PRUSSIAN
CERULEAN	KLEIN	ROYAL
COBALT	MIDNIGHT	SAPPHIRE
CYAN	NAVY	SKY
ETON	PERIWINKLE	TURQUOISE
GLAUCOUS	PERSIAN	ULTRAMARINE

PUZZLE 91: SHADES OF PINK

```
F A K A S C B N C N R C P
U R T N E R U B Y A P H P
C T E N I M R A C P E E D
H L R N E P M M L P R R O
S U K C C G L N A M S R G
I A P O U H A L M I I Y N
A L R E P S R M E R A B A
C A R N A T I O N H N L D
L G N I K C O H S S S O N
        U R H H P E R S A
        N A I L U H T S F
        R U O D A P M O P
        A S A L M O N M E
```

BRINK	FUCHSIA	SALMON
CARNATION	HOT	SHELL
CHERRY BLOSSOM	MAGENTA	SHOCKING
CORAL	PEACH	SHRIMP
CYCLAMEN	PERSIAN	THULIAN
DEEP CARMINE	POMPADOUR	ULTRA
FANDANGO	PUCE	
FRENCH ROSE	RUBY	

PUZZLE 92: BIRDS OF PREY

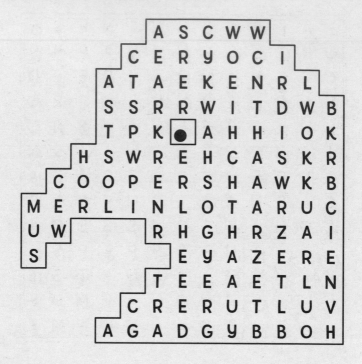

```
          A S C W W
          C E R Y O C I
        A T A E K E N R L
        S S R R W I T D W B
        T P K ● A H H I O K
        H S W R E H C A S K R
        C O O P E R S H A W K B
      M E R L I N L O T A R U C
      U W     R H G H R Z A I
      S       E Y A Z E R E
              T E E A E T L N
            C R E R U T L U V
          A G A D G Y B B O H
```

BUZZARD   KESTREL
CARACARA   KITE
CONDOR   MERLIN
COOPER'S HAWK   OSPREY
EAGLE   OWL
GREY GOSHAWK   SHIKRA
GREY HAWK   VULTURE
HOBBY

PUZZLE 93: RIVERS

```
R N I G E R L I M P O P O
M E N G O D R O D M A C D
L I T T L E B I G H O R N
A C E I N D U S C L A V O
T O E N R E O Y E I H E G
L N D L Y I Z T U V M O N
O O A O L T O T W K E N O
V E N I L E J G G E O R C
N O Z A M A S O R N E N N
O R I N O C O O R A A D O
O S B A R R O W M D N Y U
L C H U R C H I L L A D S
I S E M A H T I S I S N E
```

AMAZON	JORDAN	RIO GRANDE
BARROW	LIMPOPO	SEVERN
CAM	LITTLE BIGHORN	THAMES
CHURCHILL	MOSELLE	TWEED
CONGO	NIGER	TYNE
DORDOGNE	NILE	VOLTA
INDUS	ORINOCO	YANGTZE
ISIS	OUSE	YUKON

PUZZLE 94: DESSERTS

```
S  A  C  H  E  R  T  O  R  T  E  A  E
Y  C  B  C  S  C  O  N  E  K  K  K  D
P  R  M  A  D  E  I  R  A  C  A  K  E
L  B  T  A  N  F  P  C  A  C  C  E  C
U  L  C  S  F  B  A  E  E  B  T  B  C
M  A  O  U  A  N  U  T  R  M  U  A  L
C  C  M  R  A  P  A  R  I  C  N  N  E
A  K  F  T  S  L  H  N  Y  E  A  N  S
K  B  L  L  O  S  C  S  L  C  N  O  C
E  U  E  C  A  E  I  L  I  O  A  C  A
S  N  O  R  P  N  O  W  R  N  N  K  K
C  H  R  I  S  T  M  A  S  C  A  K  E
C  H  E  L  S  E  A  B  U  N  B  D  A
```

BANANA-NUT CAKE
BANBURY CAKE
BANNOCK
BLACK BUN
CHELSEA BUN
CHOCOLATE CAKE
CHRISTMAS CAKE
CREPE
DANISH PASTRY
ECCLES CAKE

FLAN
MADEIRA CAKE
MINCE PIE
MUFFIN
PLUM CAKE
SACHERTORTE
SCONE
STOLLEN
SULTANA CAKE
SWISS ROLL

PUZZLE 95: SCOOTER TRICKS

```
H B P O W E R S L I D E U
N E D I L S D R A O B R M
P R E F S N A R T K N A B
C U C L I F F H A N G E R
T A C A H T F K M C K E
N P B R N L A O L C C L L
A O E D E N I N V A A A L
L G B E R T O C D I I W A
P O L O W I T N K C P R F
L S L C O S V U B E L I L
L P U L A S G E B A R A I
A I S C O O T E R F L I P
W N O B A R R E L R O L L
```

AIRWALK
BANK TRANSFER
BARREL ROLL
BOARDSLIDE
BOOST
BUTTERCUP
CABDRIVER
CANNONBALL
CLIFFHANGER
FLAIR

HANDCLAP
HEEL CLICKER
LEGSWEEP
PIVOT
POGO SPIN
POWERSLIDE
SCOOTER FLIP
UMBRELLA FLIP
WALL PLANT

PUZZLE 96: WATER SPORTS

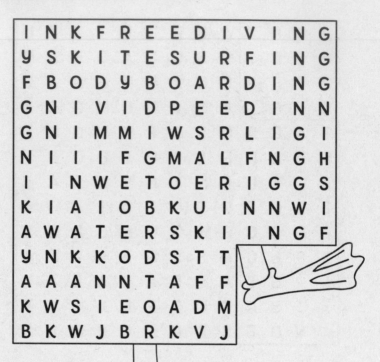

```
I  N  K  F  R  E  E  D  I  V  I  N  G
Y  S  K  I  T  E  S  U  R  F  I  N  G
F  B  O  D  Y  B  O  A  R  D  I  N  G
G  N  I  V  I  D  P  E  E  D  I  N  N
G  N  I  M  M  I  W  S  R  L  I  G  I
N  I  I  I  F  G  M  A  L  F  N  G  H
I  I  N  W  E  T  O  E  R  I  G  G  S
K  I  A  I  O  B  K  U  I  N  N  W  I
A  W  A  T  E  R  S  K  I  I  N  G  F
Y  N  K  K  O  D  S  T  T
A  A  A  N  N  T  A  F  F
K  W  S  I  E  O  A  D  M
B  K  W  J  B  R  K  V  J
```

BOATING	RAFTING
BODYBOARDING	ROWING
DEEP DIVING	SNORKELLING
FISHING	SWIMMING
FREE DIVING	WAKEBOARDING
JET-SKIING	WATERSKIING
KAYAKING	WINDSURFING
KITESURFING	

PUZZLE 97: GREEK GODS

		A	H	O	D	P	R	T	H	H
		M	D	O	S	A	S	H	A	C
		E	S	I	M	N	P	Y	B	G
		E	N	E	O	C	M	P	A	A
S	A	E	R	O	B	D	R	N	N	M	T
U	S	A	D	E	I	O	P	T	Y	O	D	T
L	C	A	P	E	N	H	H	M	U	S	A	I
O	L	P	S	U	N	A	E	C	O	B	U	S
E	E	O	S	P	N	D	U	R	E	R	O	S
A	P	L	C	A	E	E	S	A	M	I	D	A
A	I	L	T	A	M	S	A	R	L	E	T	L
T	U	O	A	S	U	E	R	E	N	M	S	T
E	S	U	T	S	E	A	H	P	E	H	E	A

ADONIS	CRONUS	HYPNOS
AEOLUS	DIONYSUS	MORPHEUS
APOLLO	EROS	NEREUS
ARES	GANYMEDE	OCEANUS
ASCLEPIUS	HADES	PAN
ATLAS	HELIOS	POSEIDON
ATTIS	HEPHAESTUS	THANATOS
BOREAS	HERMES	

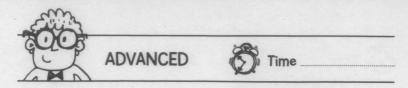
PUZZLE 98: CONSTRUCTION MACHINES

```
Y A R D E R O L L E R P G
S D B Z N T K C U R T M R
C S T A B I L I Z E R M A
R W T A C W O N S P A I D
A E B E M K U P I I C P E
P E G U A P H P R L K L R
E P W D L M E O B E S O E
R E D L E L S R E D K P D
S R T N A R D H X R I A A
C A A Y L V D O O I D V O
T R E N C H E R Z V D E L
C R O T A V A C X E E R E
D C O M P A C T O R R L D
```

BACKHOE
BULLDOZER
COMPACTOR
CRANE
DREDGER
EXCAVATOR
GRADER
LOADER
PAVER
PILE DRIVER

PIPELAYER
ROLLER
SCRAPER
SNOWCAT
STABILIZER
STEAM SHOVEL
SWEEPER
TAMPER
TRACK SKIDDER
TRENCHER

TRUCK
YARDER

PUZZLE 99: STORIES

I	T	T	I	H	Y	C	I	I	S	F	D	C
R	L	M	I	R	R	I	R	E	R	R	A	D
D	A	E	R	C	N	S	A	O	S	C	I	I
Y	C	O	V	T	H	S	M	R	T	P	E	D
V	I	H	N	O	O	A	M	O	E	T	M	M
S	R	E	I	C	N	L	N	R	H	S	I	I
F	O	A	H	C	T	C	I	R	S	O	F	O
M	T	I	E	I	K	O	I	O	I	I	Y	C
S	S	N	E	R	D	L	I	H	C	A	T	F
C	I	E	M	O	L	O	I	S	P	S	R	L
M	H	O	I	E	Y	S	A	T	N	A	F	I
R	I	Y	R	E	T	S	Y	M	Y	A	R	I
O	T	I	C	G	N	M	S	S	K	M	A	G

CHILDREN'S

CLASSIC

CRIME

FANTASY

GRAPHIC NOVEL

HISTORICAL

HORROR

MYSTERY

PERIOD

ROMANCE

SCI-FI

THRILLER

PUZZLE 100: CONSTELLATIONS

N	G	O	G	U	S	U	I	R	A	U	Q	A
O	A	S	E	I	R	A	S	D	S	S	A	R
C	S	R	M	M	R	E	E	I	U	U	A	O
S	A	U	I	N	C	M	X	I	R	E	R	N
I	G	N	N	S	O	Y	P	O	U	H	B	I
P	I	E	I	R	P	R	J	E	A	P	I	M
E	T	P	D	S	O	A	L	L	T	E	L	A
G	T	N	A	C	M	C	P	S	N	C	O	S
A	A	U	S	A	O	A	I	C	E	U	G	R
S	R	E	S	E	A	S	J	R	C	R	R	U
U	I	R	C	A	S	S	I	O	P	E	I	A
S	U	E	S	R	E	P	G	R	R	A	V	S
R	S	R	O	N	I	M	S	I	N	A	C	C

ANDROMEDA	CENTAURUS	PISCES
AQUARIUS	CEPHEUS	PYXIS
ARIES	GEMINI	SAGITTARIUS
CANIS MAJOR	LEO	SCORPIUS
CANIS MINOR	LIBRA	URSA MAJOR
CAPRICORNUS	PEGASUS	URSA MINOR
CASSIOPEIA	PERSEUS	VIRGO

PUZZLE 101: MATHS

```
I U C N D I G I T
N T A O I I T U D
F E L I A P V E U
A I C T M R A I K
C I U I E I E V S C C N G
T A L D T M Z Q E O A R F
O R A D E E T D U R R R I
R O T A R E M U N A A T B
E A I O C I I H N C L G N
A N O I T C A R T B U S E
E G N N O I S I V I D Q V
L L T C U D O R P C R I E
R E B M U N D E C I M A L
```

ADDITION	DIGIT	NUMERATOR
ANGLE	DIVISION	ODD
ARITHMETIC	DIVISOR	PRIME
AVERAGE	EQUALS	PRODUCT
BRACKET	EVEN	SUBTRACTION
CALCULATION	FACTOR	ZERO
DECIMAL	FRACTION	
DIAMETER	NUMBER	

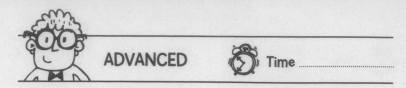

PUZZLE 102: BIG CATS

```
L P A I A O A H S L A B T
D B I R R R V T I E T I C
L S N O W L E O P A R D C
A F I S H I N G C A T O M
C S E R V A L E I E R K I
A B O B C A T D R T L D T
R O R A A O X E C N T O A
A E N C M A U A E A R K T
C C H O U A T G C H T C O
L L I T P O R D A L C U T
R R N E N R N G H R L J B
I D N U R A U G A J I I T
S E J L S O P K L Y N X H
```

BOBCAT
CARACAL
CHEETAH
COUGAR
FISHING CAT
IRIOMOTE CAT
JAGUARUNDI
KODKOD
LION
LYNX

MARGAY
OCELOT
PANTHER
PUMA
SAND CAT
SERVAL
SNOW LEOPARD
TIGER
WILDCAT

PUZZLE 103: CHESS

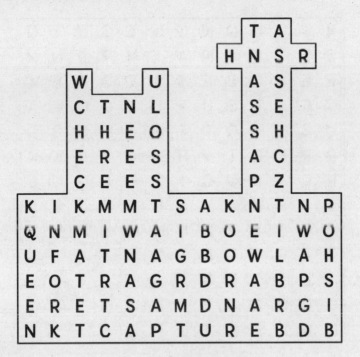

ARBITER	GRANDMASTER
BISHOP	KING
BLITZ CHESS	LOSS
CAPTURE	PAWN
CHECKMATE	QUEEN
CHESSBOARD	RANK
DRAW	ROOK
ENDGAME	TIMER
EN PASSANT	WIN
FORK	

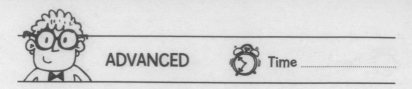

PUZZLE 104: ZOMBIES

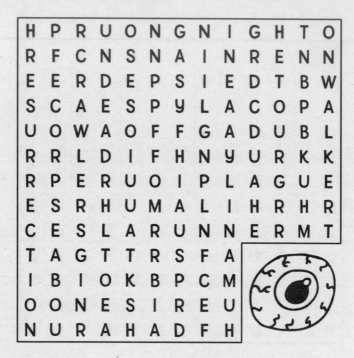

```
H P R U O N G N I G H T O
R F C N S N A I N R E N N
E E R D E P S I E D T B W
S C A E S P Y L A C O P A
U O W A O F F G A D U B L
R R L D I F H N Y U R K K
R P E R U O I P L A G U E
E S R H U M A L I H R H R
C E S L A R U N N E R M T
T A G T T R S F A
I B I O K B P C M
O O N E S I R E U
N U R A H A D F H
```

ANIMATION

APOCALYPSE

BODY PART

BRAINS

CORPSE

CRAWLER

GHOUL

HUMAN

LURKER

NIGHT

ONSLAUGHT

PLAGUE

RESURRECTION

RISEN

RUNNER

SHUFFLER

TERRIFYING

UNDEAD

WALKER

PUZZLE 105: WORLD FOODS

```
A E O J E N I O D E C A M
A R E T R U F K N A R F I
T L I T U H A C M Z C D I
A G J U J O H L A Z L R G
N A A O A I O A I I U O G
O D H G L D K D Y P B B C
R O B A B A G A N O U S H
E G D R S A B O I L R A O
P A I S S M A J H E R G P
E D U O A O T I S N I R S
P O M M C F F E U T T O U
M A I A O M O F S A O M E
S U T U A R K R E U A S Y
```

BABA GANOUSH	GADO-GADO	POLENTA
BHAJI	IMAM BAYILDI	RAGOUT
BURRITO	KOFTA	SAMOSA
CHOP SUEY	MACEDOINE	SAUERKRAUT
DOLMA	MOUSSAKA	SMORGASBORD
ENCHILADA	PEPERONATA	SUSHI
FEIJOADA	PILAU	TACO
FRANKFURTER	PIZZA	

PUZZLE 106: FAMOUS QUEENS

```
N T B N E N I L O R A C E
E G U I N E V E R E C D I
L I A S A B M A R Y C E N
E N O H P E S R E P I A A
H Y E R G E N A J Y D A L
P T A F T A H N I L U R A
R E E I E I B S A E O T K
T V N B R R T E T B B A O
H O R E A O T A H A P P U
      L Z T I N S H O I
      B O I C T I S E L
      I P P L I I A L I
      Y I T E E V L C L
```

ANNE	LADY JANE GREY
BOUDICCA	LILIUOKALANI
CAROLINE	MARY
CLEOPATRA	NEFERTITI
ELIZABETH	PENELOPE
GUINEVERE	PERSEPHONE
HATSHEPSUT	SHEBA
HELEN	TITANIA
ISABEL	VICTORIA

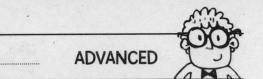

PUZZLE 107: LONDON TRAIN STATIONS

```
I R S R A I R F K C A L B
E T A G R O O M A N U L L
G B E L L I N G H A M E A
W A T E R L O O E A S T C
E G D I R B N O D N O L K
U M E A S T D U L W I C H
S L K I N G S C R O S S E
T F P A D D I N G T O N A
O M A R Y L E B O N E M T
N O D A O R L E G N A L H
B F A R R I N G D O N K H
Y T S S S T P A N C R A S
S S O R C G N I R A H C C
```

ANGEL ROAD
BELLINGHAM
BLACKFRIARS
BLACKHEATH
CANNON STREET
CHARING CROSS
EAST DULWICH
EUSTON

FARRINGDON
KING'S CROSS
LONDON BRIDGE
MARYLEBONE
MOORGATE
PADDINGTON
ST PANCRAS
WATERLOO EAST

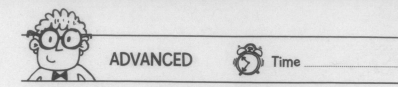

PUZZLE 108: FAMILY MEMBERS

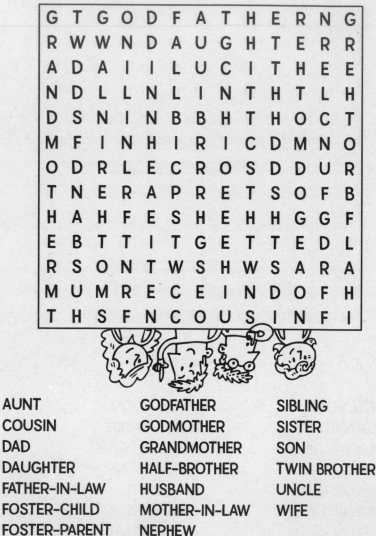

```
G T G O D F A T H E R N G
R W W N D A U G H T E R R
A D A I I L U C I T H E E
N D L L N L I N T H T L H
D S N I N B B H T H O C T
M F I N H I R I C D M N O
O D R L E C R O S D D U R
T N E R A P R E T S O F B
H A H F E S H E H H G G F
E B T T I T G E T T E D L
R S O N T W S H W S A R A
M U M R E C E I N D O F H
T H S F N C O U S I N F I
```

AUNT	GODFATHER	SIBLING
COUSIN	GODMOTHER	SISTER
DAD	GRANDMOTHER	SON
DAUGHTER	HALF-BROTHER	TWIN BROTHER
FATHER-IN-LAW	HUSBAND	UNCLE
FOSTER-CHILD	MOTHER-IN-LAW	WIFE
FOSTER-PARENT	NEPHEW	
GODCHILD	NIECE	

PUZZLE 109: TREES

```
M T R G H N M O E P F I R
A A I E E M T U N O C O C
N F I P D P S S A W T E W
O M S O U L U P E U U C M
T A A P U A E W R S N O A
S U I P F Q I P O E T O G
O N N E L L E M M C S M N
E O A L L E L S A U E Y O
S N A O A P E N C R H C L
F A W K E W P I Y P C A I
A O M L E L A A S S R E A
O S U T P Y L A C U E M R
F C H N M L A P E U L E E
```

APPLE   MAGNOLIA
ASH   MAPLE
ASPEN   OAK
CHESTNUT   PALM
COCONUT   PINE
ELDER   SEQUOIA
ELM   SPRUCE
EUCALYPTUS   SYCAMORE
FIG   WALNUT
FIR   WILLOW

PUZZLE 110: BERRIES

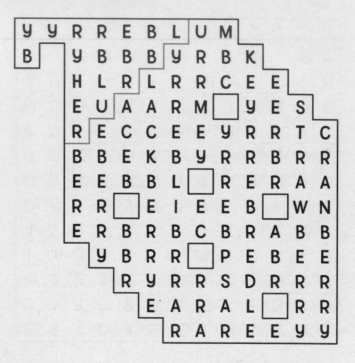

```
Y Y R R E B L U M
B   Y B B B Y R B K
    H L R L R R C E E
    E U A A R M   Y E S
    R E C C E E Y R T C
    B B E K B Y R R B R R
    E E B B L   R E R A A
    R R   E I E E B   W N
    E R B R B C B R A B B
      Y B R R   P E B E E
      R Y R R S D R R
        E A R A L   R R
        R A R E E Y Y
```

BILBERRY
BLACKBERRY
BLUEBERRY
CRANBERRY
ELDERBERRY
HUCKLEBERRY
MULBERRY
RASPBERRY
STRAWBERRY

PUZZLE 111: SWIMMING

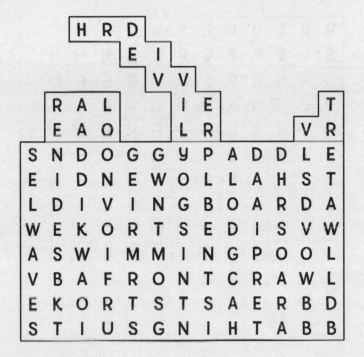

	H	R	D							
		E	I							
		V	V							
R	A	L		I	E					T
E	A	O		L	R			V	R	
S	N	D	O	G	G	Y	P	A	D	D	L	E
E	I	D	N	E	W	O	L	L	A	H	S	T
L	D	I	V	I	N	G	B	O	A	R	D	A
W	E	K	O	R	T	S	E	D	I	S	V	W
A	S	W	I	M	M	I	N	G	P	O	O	L
V	B	A	F	R	O	N	T	C	R	A	W	L
E	K	O	R	T	S	T	S	A	E	R	B	D
S	T	I	U	S	G	N	I	H	T	A	B	B

BATHING SUIT	RIVER
BREASTSTROKE	SEA
DIVE	SHALLOW END
DIVING BOARD	SIDESTROKE
DOGGY–PADDLE	SWIMMING POOL
FRONT CRAWL	WATER
LANE	WAVES
LIDO	

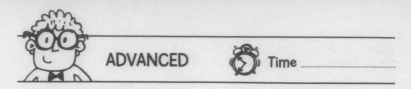
PUZZLE 112: FAST FOOD

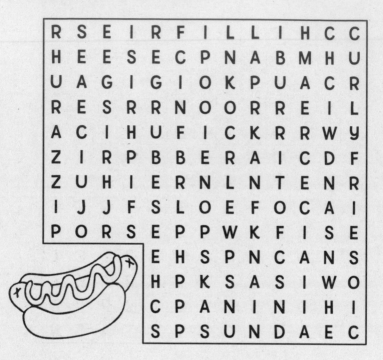

```
R S E I R F I L L I H C C
H E E S E C P N A B M H U
U A G I G I O K P U A C R
R E S R R N O O R R E I L
A C I H U F I C K R R W Y
Z I R P B B E R A I C D F
Z U H I E R N L N T E N R
I J J F S L O E F O C A I
P O R S E P P W K F I S E
        E H S P N C A N S
        H P K S A S I W O
        C P A N I N I H I
        S P S U N D A E C
```

APPLE PIE	ICE CREAM
BURRITO	JUICE
CHEESEBURGER	ONION RINGS
CHICKEN BURGER	PANINI
CHILLI FRIES	PIZZA
COOKIE	SANDWICH
CRISPS	SUNDAE
CURLY FRIES	TACO
HASH BROWNS	WAFFLE FRIES

PUZZLE 113: HERBS AND SPICES

```
B A S I L I Q U O R I C E
D R O S E M A R Y I H O W
O K L Y S W H T C I L A N
O E A E U A O T V A T N O
W E C F N S R E H E D I G
M R I M F N S G R Y D S A
R G R R I I E C N I M E R
O U E L D E R F L O W E R
W N M A T E A L C E M D A
Y E R K S N D H I U T E T
D F U S K A I E D M M E L
R H T E J A S M I N E I B
S R E P A C H I C O R Y N
```

ALOE	DILL	LIQUORICE
ANISEED	ELDERFLOWER	MINT
BASIL	FENNEL	ROSEMARY
BETEL	FENUGREEK	TARRAGON
CAPERS	HORSERADISH	THYME
CHICORY	JASMINE	TURMERIC
CHIVES	KAFFIR LIME	WATERCRESS
CUMIN	LEMON GRASS	WORMWOOD

PUZZLE 114: TOOL BOX

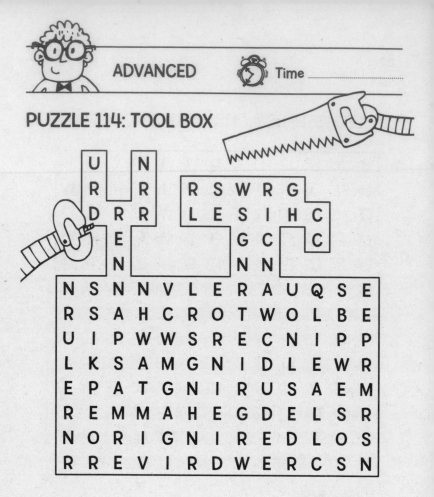

```
  U     N
  R     R         R S W R G
  D R R         L E S I H C
  E R             G C           C
  E               N C
N S N N V L E R A U Q S E
R S A H C R O T W O L B E E
U I P W W S R E C N I P P
L K S A M G N I D L E W R
E P A T G N I R U S A E M
R E M M A H E G D E L S R
N O R I G N I R E D L O S
R R E V I R D W E R C S N
```

BLOWTORCH

CHISEL

MEASURING TAPE

NAIL

PINCERS

PLUNGER

RULER

SAW

SCREWDRIVER

SLEDGEHAMMER

SOLDERING IRON

SPANNER

SQUARE

WELDING MASK

WRENCH

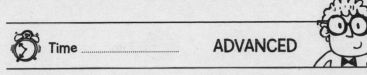
PUZZLE 115: SHERLOCK HOLMES CHARACTERS

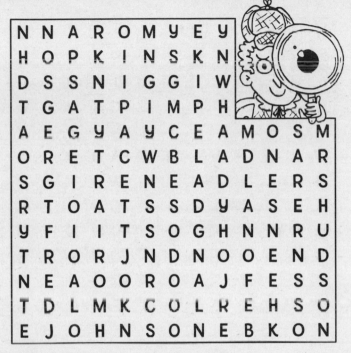

```
N N A R O M Y E Y
H O P K I N S K N
D S S N I G G I W
T G A T P I M P H
A E Y A Y C E A M O S M
O R E T C W B L A D N A R
S G I R E N E A D L E R S
R T O A T S S D Y A S E H
Y F I I T S O G H N N R U
T R O R J N D N O O E N D
N E A O O R O A J F E S S
T D L M K C O L R E H S O
E J O H N S O N E B K O N
```

BAYNES
BRADSTREET
GREGSON
HOPKINS
IRENE ADLER
JOHNSON
JONES
LANGDALE PIKE
LESTRADE

MARY
MORAN
MORIARTY
MRS HUDSON
MYCROFT
SHERLOCK
WATSON
WIGGINS

PUZZLE 116: FAMOUS AUTHORS

```
N T S E T N A V R E C T M
R R T C A R R O L L R O E
E R E Y S C O N R A D L C
L I V O T T L L R S Y B W
B G E J N E I K L O T E V
W Y N D H A M B D O O C A
N D S I M A U R S B P K R
H R O C M R D P A E K E C
E A N K G E R L P N N T H
N H N E T O L S T O Y T E
R I S N U A T F K E J T R
R S C S R T L N A H C U B
V P T D A C N L D T R H L
```

AMIS	DICKENS	TOLSTOY
ARCHER	DOYLE	TROLLOPE
BALLARD	FLEMING	WYNDHAM
BECKETT	HARDY	
BUCHAN	JOYCE	
BURGESS	NESBIT	
CARROLL	PROUST	
CERVANTES	STEVENSON	
CONRAD	TOLKIEN	

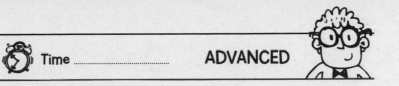

PUZZLE 117: BOATS

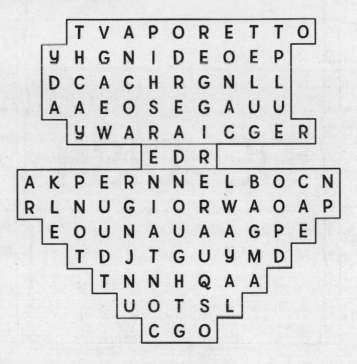

CANOE	JUNK
COBLE	PEDALO
CONTAINER SHIP	PUNT
CUTTER	SAMPAN
DHOW	SQUARE-RIGGER
DINGHY	TUG
DREADNOUGHT	VAPORETTO
GONDOLA	YACHT
GULET	YAWL

PUZZLE 118: FRUITS

```
E P G Q P Y K N L P
C L E M E N T I N E
W Y Y T S N T L W N
E E R M A N G O O I
B T R A T N L I D R
T E E S S M A O R A N G E E S
W H H T U P T R E T T L P M R
W R C R M A B L G C D E G I E
A L I A A T P E E E H C Y L K
N L O W E P R P R N M E R U A
A E A B A P A B N R N O M E L
N O L E M R E T A W Y Q P P L
A R N R G R P A E P U C P G E
B I Y R R E B K C A L B A E O
P E E Y R U W E T A N W N W A
```

BANANA
BLACKBERRY
CHERRY
CLEMENTINE
DATE
ELDERBERRY
GRAPE
KIWI

KUMQUAT
LEMON
LIME
LYCHEE
MANGO
NECTARINE
ORANGE
PEACH

PEAR
PINEAPPLE
POMEGRANATE
RASPBERRY
SATSUMA
STRAWBERRY
WATERMELON

PUZZLE 119: SOLAR SYSTEM

C	F	U	L	R	S	D	Y	J	U	P	I	T	E	R
R	E	R	C	U	E	A	U	H	I	A	S	T	R	T
U	R	R	N	Y	W	T	T	O	T	U	R	T	I	H
E	U	A	E	Y	L	T	K	U	L	R	U	T	S	A
R	R	P	K	S	U	N	E	V	R	C	A	M	M	U
U	D	L	A	S						N	T	E	I	M
R	I	U	M	O						O	N	R	N	E
M	O	T	E	L						R	E	C	O	A
R	R	O	K	A						B	C	U	R	O
P	E	T	A	R						I	M	R	P	T
R	T	E	M	W	R	E	M	C	A	T	L	Y	L	C
T	S	M	A	I	T	E	T	I	L	L	E	T	A	S
E	A	O	N	N	O	K	E	N	U	T	P	E	N	K
M	I	C	U	D	W	A	R	F	P	L	A	N	E	T
E	B	I	C	K	U	I	P	E	R	B	E	L	T	U

ASTEROID
CENTAURS
CERES
COMET
DWARF PLANET
EARTH
ERIS
HAUMEA

JUPITER
KUIPER BELT
MAKEMAKE
MERCURY
MILKY WAY
MINOR PLANET
NEPTUNE
OORT CLOUD

ORBIT
PLUTO
SATELLITE
SATURN
SOLAR WIND
TITAN
URANUS
VENUS

PUZZLE 120: INSECTS

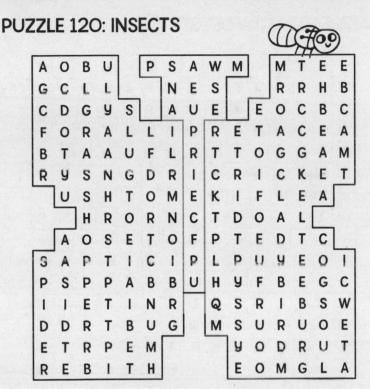

```
A O B U   P S A W M   M T E E
G C L L   N E S   R R H B
C D G Y S   A U E   E O C B C
F O R A L L I   P R E T A C E A
B T A A U F L R T T O G G A M
R Y S N G D R I C R I C K E T
  U S H T O M E K I F L E A
    H R O R N C T D O A L
    A O S E T O F P T E D T C
S A P T I C I P L P U Y E O I
P S P P A B B U H Y F B E G C
I I E T I N R   Q S R I B S W
D D R T B U G   M S U R U O E
E T R P E M   Y O D R U T
R E B I T H   E O M G L A
```

ANT	DRAGONFLY	MOTH
BEETLE	FLEA	SLUG
BUG	GNAT	SNAIL
BUTTERFLY	GRASSHOPPER	SPIDER
CATERPILLAR	GRUB	TERMITE
CENTIPEDE	LADYBIRD	WASP
COCKROACH	MAGGOT	WORM
CRICKET	MOSQUITO	

PUZZLE 121: RAINFORESTS

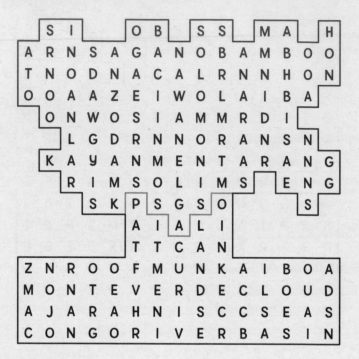

BIAK-NUMFOOR

BIALOWIEZA

CONGO RIVER BASIN

GONDWANA

HOH

KAYAN MENTARANG

LACANDON

MONTEVERDE CLOUD

OLYMPIC

SAGANO BAMBOO

SERAM

SINHARAJA

SOLOMON ISLANDS

TASMANIAN

TONGASS

PUZZLE 122: ANCIENT EGYPT

```
              K
           I  F  S
        F  S  I  H  I
        L  D  R  T  P  O  L
     O  E  I  H  I  Y  L  B  E
     O  E  S  E  O  T  L  E  Y  O  B
     D  R  O  B  E  A  R  G  E  V  C  E  O
  D  T  R  E  Y  M  R  E  O  S  L  A  V  E  S
  C  I  S  M  U  I  A  F  R  S  C  R  I  B  E
  N  H  M  L  A  L  H  F  E  S  M  T  R  H  R
  U  U  E  A  F  O  P  N  I  M  H  O  T  E  P
  M  T  S  A  R  C  O  P  H  A  G  U  S  L  E
  A  D  N  U  D  Y  N  A  S  T  Y  C  M  I  E
  U  K  S  A  S  E  P  H  C  S  P  H  I  N  X
  H  S  F  A  F  T  E  R  L  I  F  E  O  I  S
```

AFTERLIFE	HIEROGLYPH	PYRAMID
AMULET	IMHOTEP	REEDS
AMUN	MUMMY	SARCOPHAGUS
ANKH	NEFERTITI	SCRIBE
CARTOUCHE	NILE	SLAVES
DYNASTY	OBELISK	SPHINX
EYE OF HORUS	OSIRIS	THEBES
FLOOD	PHARAOH	

PUZZLE 123: MUSICAL INSTRUMENTS

```
G I N A G R O H T U O M D R D
A R H F R E N C H H O R N N B
E U I L L E A N P I P E S S E
H L E I P S N E K C O L G O O
D R O H C I V A L C L T S N D
H M E L O D E O N E D S C R A
U N N Z N E O R B I A I O O N
R A O G I Z O R D B O H R H I
D R H I A S A G E D C W A L T
Y H P K D L E L N I C E N E R
G D A U U R B H S O L E G G E
U O S B I U O P T G B N L U C
R B U D O K R C U N S A A L N
D T O D M A O B C D Y W I F O
Y O S I H R O J N A B S S D C
```

ACCORDION
BANJO
BONGO
BUGLE
CELLO
CLAVICHORD
CONCERTINA
DIDGERIDOO
DOUBLE BASS

FLUGELHORN
FRENCH HORN
GLOCKENSPIEL
HARPSICHORD
HURDY-GURDY
KAZOO
MELODEON
MOUTH ORGAN
SWANEE WHISTLE

SYNTHESIZER
TUBULAR BELLS

PUZZLE 124: SHAKESPEARE PLAYS

```
A T S R L K I N G L E A R C C
C H U H A A U T E O S H O Y T
A G N E G I H I S E E M M I N
R I A N O I R G L N E B E H H
H N L R I B Y C R D E K O H T
E H O Y H N I Y Y L I J A T E
N T I I R R V O I L G M N K B
R F R V E I F N U L T D H C
Y L O P E E O I E R G J R A
V E C A R R Y K T H S E U T M
I W R R A S E A C S U I L U J
I T O T A R I C H A R D I I I
I R T I M O N O F A T H E N S
S U C I N O R D N A S U T I T
E E L A T S R E T N I W V A Y
```

AS YOU LIKE IT	KING LEAR
COMEDY OF ERRORS	MACBETH
CORIOLANUS	PERICLES
CYMBELINE	RICHARD III
HAMLET	ROMEO AND JULIET
HENRY IV PART II	TIMON OF ATHENS
HENRY VIII	TITUS ANDRONICUS
HENRY VI PART I	TWELFTH NIGHT
JULIUS CAESAR	WINTER'S TALE
KING JOHN	

PUZZLE 125: DINOSAURS

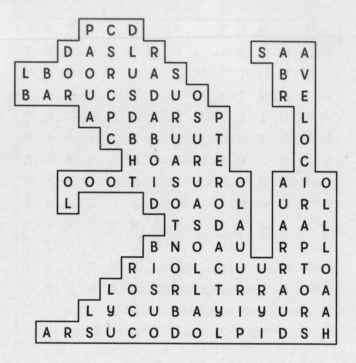

```
      P C D
    D A S L R              S A A
  L B O O R U A S          B V
  B A R U C S D U O        R E
    A P D A R S P            L
    C B B U U T              O
    H O A R E                C
  O O O T I S U R O        A I O
  L     D O A O L          U R L
        T S D A            A A L
        B N O A U          R P L
      R I O L C U U R T    T O
    L O S R L T R R A O    A A
    L Y C U B A Y I Y U R A
  A R S U C O D O L P I D S H
```

ALLOSAURUS
BRACHIOSAURUS
BRONTOSAURUS
DIPLODOCUS
PTERODACTYL
VELOCIRAPTOR

PUZZLE 126: US PRESIDENTS

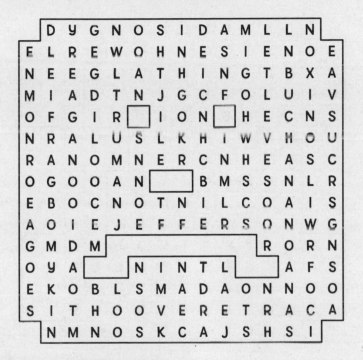

D Y G N O S I D A M L L N
E L R E W O H N E S I E N O E
N E E G L A T H I N G T B X A
M I A D T N J G C F O L U I V
O F G I R   I O N   H E C N S
N R A L U S L K H I W V H O U
R A N O M N E R C N H E A S C
O G O O A N   B M S S N L R
E B O C N O T N I L C O A I S
A O I E J E F F E R S O N W G
G M D M   R O R N
O Y A   N I N T L   A F S
E K O B L S M A D A O N N O O
S I T H O O V E R E T R A C A
N M N O S K C A J S H S I

ADAMS	HOOVER	MONROE
BUCHANAN	JACKSON	NIXON
CARTER	JEFFERSON	OBAMA
CLINTON	JOHNSON	REAGAN
COOLIDGE	KENNEDY	ROOSEVELT
EISENHOWER	LINCOLN	TRUMAN
GARFIELD	MADISON	WASHINGTON
GRANT	MCKINLEY	WILSON

PUZZLE 127: MOTOR RACING

```
      T A E H C D A C A D R
  T O I K T N O I S N E P S U S
  H G A L F D E R E U Q E H C T
  E R R B H T H G I A R T S X E
  B S E U P G I G E A E E I M W
      E R P E N N C D R R H
      T N E D R I F T P S R
      S O D K N T Y D A P O
      R U A G R R N F E O L
      E T L O E A E F I I L
  I X D I S W R T M D A L C A T
  B A N K A G Y S A K T E A M T
  D E U L E C T R E S C R G U D
  J B L E A K C A J R I A E U Q
      W R E E T S R E V O B
```

AIR JACK	PEDALS	STRAIGHT
BACKMARKER	QUALIFYING	SUSPENSION
BANK	RACING LINE	TEAM
BRAKE	RADIO	TYRE WALL
BURNOUT	ROLL CAGE	UNDERSTEER
CHEQUERED FLAG	SAFETY CAR	WETS
DRIFT	SPOILER	
GRAND PRIX	STARTING GRID	
HEAT		
OVERSTEER		

PUZZLE 128: VOLCANOES

```
        P I L N S B   R I
        O S A N T O R I N I
      G A L E R A S O A A
      K M O D       E
    E M M I L I
    H M B O S J A E
    T O R U U T A A T
  Y L N T F C N H R T
  I A T N E Z N U E U K
  Y O K S V E H C U Y L K
  R U H E P A U R I M E E A
G N Y I R A G O N G O A T N S
K J Y A R I G A R U M A Y N S
A A E U A L I K R A K A T O A
P I N A T U B O R U L A W U N
```

ETNA	NYIRAGONGO	UNZEN
FUJI	PINATUBO	
GALERAS	RUAPEHU	
HEKLA	SAKURAJIMA	
KILAUEA	SANTORINI	
KLYUCHEVSKOY	ST HELENS	
KRAKATOA	STROMBOLI	
MAYON	TAAL	
MONTSERRAT	TEIDE	
NYAMURAGIRA	ULAWUN	

PUZZLE 129: GREEK ALPHABET

D	S	T	P	U	M	G	M	A	M	I	H	C	I	T
M	E	M	O	B	C	A	O	O	T	A	A	M	S	K
P	L	M	A	A	M	M	I	I	O	E	M	T	I	S
H	A	T	T	G	I	N	I	P	A	U	H	M	C	T
I	E	T	I	C	I	A	O	T	A	R	A	T	A	D
B	A	S	R	L	E	O	L	L	O	H	O	T	U	G
L	A	O	H	T	I	E	A	C	I	K	E	A	O	D
A	N	B	N	A	D	D	O	A	A	S	A	L	O	S
O	M	P	A	O	B	S	U	P	R	A	P	O	B	E
Z	E	G	L	M	A	P	P	G	H	O	M	E	G	A
E	H	O	A	M	S	A	T	A	O	L	E	M	T	T
T	N	L	T	I	A	A	R	I	A	O	I	M	O	D
A	R	L	L	P	A	O	T	U	T	M	O	C	A	O
P	I	O	A	L	P	H	A	P	I	S	T	S	I	O
T	N	A	M	O	O	A	I	A	I	A	A	H	U	L

ALPHA	**OMEGA**
BETA	**OMICRON**
CHI	**PHI**
DELTA	**RHO**
EPSILON	**SIGMA**
GAMMA	**TAU**
IOTA	**THETA**
KAPPA	**UPSILON**
LAMBDA	**ZETA**

PUZZLE 130: MUSIC TERMS

```
R  C  N  O  I  T  A  R  T  S  E  H  C  R  O
T  E  M  I  T  R  U  O  F  E  E  R  H  T  I
L  A  V  R  E  T  N  I  T  C  E  F  R  E  P
L  A  R  A  T  A  E  B  N  W  O  D  N  I  A
E  U  V  S  U  C  L  A  E  U  I  I  A  R  C
A  N  O  R  A  Q  N  L  R  R  L  N  U  I  C
D  O  I  V  E  O  I  F  E  R  O  T  B  N  I
I  O  I  L  S  T  O  M  A  P  A  C  A  F  A
N  V  L  S  R  U  N  B  E  I  P  T  S  O  C
C  O  I  O  R  E  E  I  G  S  U  A  S  R  C
N  D  S  T  R  L  G  G  R  R  I  C  C  Z  A
O  R  I  I  B  O  O  D  A  O  I  M  L  A  T
T  M  A  U  N  P  S  L  E  R  J  S  E  N  U
E  C  O  A  P  U  I  O  U  L  I  A  F  D  R
O  D  N  A  T  N  E  L  L  A  R  E  M  O  A
```

A CAPPELLA
APPOGGIATURA
BASS CLEF
DEMISEMIQUAVER
DISSONANCE
DOLOROSO
DOUBLE BAR LINE

DOWNBEAT
FOUR-FOUR TIME
LEADING NOTE
LEDGER LINE
LYRIC
MAJOR INTERVAL
NATURAL

ORCHESTRATION
PERFECT INTERVAL
PIANO
SCORE
THREE-FOUR TIME
UNISON
VIVACE

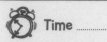

PUZZLE 131: FAMOUS SCIENTISTS

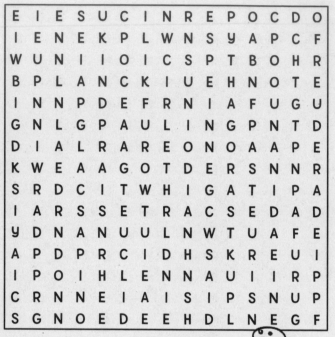

E	I	E	S	U	C	I	N	R	E	P	O	C	D	O
I	E	N	E	K	P	L	W	N	S	Y	A	P	C	F
W	U	N	I	I	O	I	C	S	P	T	B	O	H	R
B	P	L	A	N	C	K	I	U	E	H	N	O	T	E
I	N	N	P	D	E	F	R	N	I	A	F	U	G	U
G	N	L	G	P	A	U	L	I	N	G	P	N	T	D
D	I	A	L	R	A	R	E	O	N	O	A	A	P	E
K	W	E	A	A	G	O	T	D	E	R	S	N	N	R
S	R	D	C	I	T	W	H	I	G	A	T	I	P	A
I	A	R	S	S	E	T	R	A	C	S	E	D	A	D
Y	D	N	A	N	U	U	L	N	W	T	U	A	F	E
A	P	D	P	R	C	I	D	H	S	K	R	E	U	I
I	P	O	I	H	L	E	N	N	A	U	I	I	R	P
C	R	N	N	E	I	A	I	S	I	P	S	N	U	P
S	G	N	O	E	D	E	E	H	D	L	N	E	G	F

BOHR
COPERNICUS
CURIE
DARWIN
DESCARTES
EINSTEIN
EUCLID
FARADAY
FREUD
GALILEO

HAWKING
KEPLER
LAGRANGE
NEWTON
PASCAL
PASTEUR
PAULING
PLANCK
PYTHAGORAS
TURING

PUZZLE 132: FAMOUS INVENTORS

```
A E U A B I G E M R B I R O M
B N O D O N U C E I V B O L R
B N O O H A T B M E M E A F I
R Y B E L M E E O E D E R B S
A W A I I T N L R E N A I R I
I M S D N S B L S N N S J I C
L A E A O A E R E K I U A O E
L R D V L E R C L S D R I Y S
E C E I I E G I S S U D E O L
E O M N K A N U O B I S A E L
E N I C A S A N I C D E S D U
L I H I L R E K K R D E O I B
O N C R T S G S I G I E U S O
C I R S N A O B B D M I V O L
I E A K N N B A B B A G E N Y
```

ARCHIMEDES
BABBAGE
BELL
BIRDSEYE
BIRO
BOHLIN
BRAILLE
COLE

DA VINCI
DICKSON
DIESEL
EASTMAN
EDISON
FRANKLIN
GUTENBERG
JUDSON

LAENNEC
MARCONI
MORSE
RUBIK
STRAUSS
WYNNE

PUZZLE 133: CLOUDS

ALTOCUMULUS
ARCUS
CIRROSTRATUS
CIRRUS
CUMULOGENITUS
CUMULONIMBUS
FIBRATUS
INCUS
INTORTUS

LACUNOSUS
OPACUS
PILEUS
PYROCUMULUS
STRATOCUMULUS
UNCINUS
UNDULATUS
VELUM

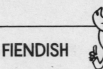

PUZZLE 134: ELEMENTS

```
L N Y M U I M O R H C P E R U
A N E G O R D Y H N H N M E N
P O O E M T E X E O L I U N Y
L O N R I U E X S U O T I I N
A I T M O N I P E E R R N R O
I M I A U B H N N B I O A O M
I U U N S O N I A E N G T U I
N I N I R S M M G R E E I L T
U D G U S O I N N Y U N T F N
M N G M R T I U A L E N O S A
N A T B N C N S M L
I C E R K O U G E I
A S N E B T R S A U
M A L U M I N I U M
M U I L L A G M N S
```

ALUMINIUM	GALLIUM	PLATINUM
ANTIMONY	GERMANIUM	POTASSIUM
BERYLLIUM	HYDROGEN	SCANDIUM
BORON	MAGNESIUM	SELENIUM
BROMINE	MANGANESE	TITANIUM
CHLORINE	NICKEL	TUNGSTEN
CHROMIUM	NITROGEN	URANIUM
FLUORINE	PHOSPHORUS	XENON

PUZZLE 135: GEOLOGICAL TIME PERIODS

```
D A C O C I S S A R U J I S S
N S C E N O Z O I C A S M T T
N P E H E A B C I S S A I R T
C A R B O N I F E R O U S N O
I L I E V L E R P I E E S N D
O A I N C Y O C U C S O I C E
Z E E H A A R C O L J A S R V
O O L N T V M A E I I E S E O
E C E E E L B N N L S I T N
A E P P I C R Y R R E P P A I
L N E N E C O T S I E L P C A
A E I I N Y I G I N A T I E N
P O R D O V I C I A N N A O I
Y C I O Z O S E M L R E N U O
S O N A I M R E P N O Y P S Q
```

CARBONIFEROUS	MISSISSIPPIAN	PLEISTOCENE
CENOZOIC	OLIGOCENE	PLIOCENE
CRETACEOUS	ORDOVICIAN	PRECAMBRIAN
DEVONIAN	PALAEOCENE	QUATERNARY
HOLOCENE	PALAEOZOIC	SILURIAN
JURASSIC	PENNSYLVANIAN	TERTIARY
MESOZOIC	PERMIAN	TRIASSIC

PUZZLE 136: GREEK HEROES

```
E O S P Y L A C S N P N L T S
N N T S C S T S N E R I S N C
D R N S U H N L N L T B N O C
S S A D T U A E P E O A C N A
P H E R C U L E S H R Y O M D
M M E S L O A O N C C H U E M
T S D U P A T N I L P B O M U
C U I E O S A S O O O S O A S
I E O S D N S P R G A U I G I
T S M R U U S E T O R R U A E
S E E E S U L C O R T A P B S
U H D P S L P N T E Y C I R I
U T E L E M A C H U S I E E R
N S S B U N O S A J E N S H B
E A O L S E L L I H C A S J E
```

ACHILLES	CYCLOPS	NARCISSUS
AGAMEMNON	DIOMEDES	ODYSSEUS
ARGONAUTS	HECTOR	PATROCLUS
ATALANTA	HELEN	PENELOPE
BELLEROPHON	HERCULES	PERSEUS
BRISEIS	ICARUS	SIRENS
CADMUS	JASON	TELEMACHUS
CALYPSO	MEDUSA	THESEUS

PUZZLE 137: HORSE BREEDS

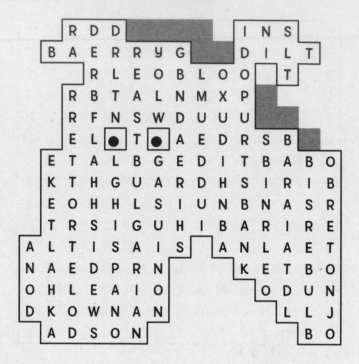

AKHAL-TEKE	EAST BULGARIAN	OLDENBURG
ARAB	EINSIEDLER	SHIRE
AUXOIS	HISPANO	SWEDISH HALFBRED
BARB	IRISH DRAUGHT	TRAIT DU NORD
BRETON	JUTLAND	WALER
BRUMBY	KNABSTRUP	
DOLE TROTTER	LOKAI	
DON	NONIUS	

PUZZLE 138: SHAPES

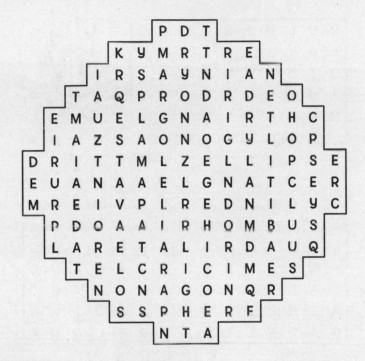

```
            P D T
        K Y M R T R E
        I R S A Y N I A N
    T A Q P R O D R D E O
  E M U E L G N A I R T H C
    I A Z S A O N O G Y L O P
D R I T T M L Z E L L I P S E
  E U A N A A E L G N A T C E R
  M R E I V P L R E D N I L Y C
    P D O A A I R H O M B U S
    L A R E T A L I R D A U Q
      T E L C R I C I M E S
      N O N A G O N Q R
        S S P H E R F
          N T A
```

CONE
CYLINDER
DIAMOND
ELLIPSE
HEART
KITE
NONAGON
OVAL
PARALLELOGRAM
PENTAGON

POLYGON
PYRAMID
QUADRILATERAL
RECTANGLE
RHOMBUS
SEMICIRCLE
SPHERE
SQUARE
STAR
TRAPEZIUM

TRAPEZOID
TRIANGLE

PUZZLE 139: SHADES OF RED

```
R  U  L  M  A  R  O  O  N  S
L  A  V  A  T  N  E  G  A  M
O  T  O  I  N  O  S  D  D  E
A  U  R  R  N  I  T  C  W  N
N  N  O  G  Q  L  D  A  A  O
Y  T  S  N  S  L  S  R  N  R  O  L  A  Y  M
E  S  E  A  O  I  O  N  A  O  L  D  W  D  M
A  E  W  S  H  M  N  E  W  C  S  E  M  N  A
Y  H  O  M  M  R  M  L  E  N  O  M  T  U  A
Y  C  O  Q  U  E  L  I  C  O  T  N  I  G  B
E  B  D  B  M  V  R  A  S  P  B  E  R  R  Y
A  N  U  A  F  H  T  N  A  R  A  M  A  U  C
L  A  L  R  C  A  R  M  I  N  E  C  A  B  O
A  F  N  E  A  T  S  S  I  N  O  P  I  A  A
G  A  R  N  E  T  E  S  I  R  E  C  R  N  A
```

AMARANTH	COQUELICOT	RASPBERRY
AUBURN	CRIMSON	REDWOOD
BURGUNDY	FLAME	ROSEWOOD
CARDINAL	GARNET	RUBY
CARMINE	LAVA	SANGRIA
CARNELIAN	MAGENTA	SCARLET
CERISE	MAROON	SINOPIA
CHESTNUT	PERSIMMON	VERMILLION

PUZZLE 140: SHADES OF GREEN

```
        I O M N V N R E H N
        I M Y M U E D N E E
        F E R N V E A E V E
        O N T O S R R E I R
        R I L U A G T R L O
Y N A I E E C E S N R M G O A
N E F N M S R P I S E O E K N
P O E D E T A U S U T U L R N
E F D I R R Q O N O N T G A O
S O E A A E M I L G U H N D J
T L H G L P E E J N H G U I H
A C U R D E P J A E D R J R M
G S A E D A C L D O T E A L E
T H A E Q R U W E D Y E N O H
E L E N A I D I R I V N M E O
```

APPLE   FERN   LIME

ASPARAGUS   FOREST   MINT

CELADON   HARLEQUIN   MOSS

CHARTREUSE   GREEN   MYRTLE

CLOVER   HONEYDEW   PEAR

DARK OLIVE   HUNTER GREEN   TEAL

DARTMOUTH   INDIA GREEN   VIRIDIAN

GREEN   JADE

EMERALD   JUNGLE GREEN

PUZZLE 141: PASTA

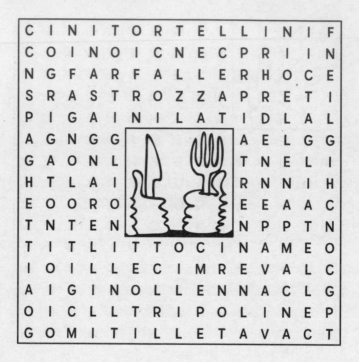

```
C I N I T O R T E L L I N I F
C O I N O I C N E C P R I I N
N G F A R F A L L E R H O C E
S R A S T R O Z Z A P R E T I
P I G A I N I L A T I D L A L
A G N G G         A E L G G
G A O N L         T N E L I
H T L A I         R N N I H
E O O R O         E E A A C
T N T E N         N P P T N
T I T L I T T O C I N A M E O
I O I L L E C I M R E V A L C
A I G I N O L L E N N A C L G
O I C L L T R I P O L I N E P
G O M I T I L L E T A V A C T
```

AGNOLOTTI	FIORI	SPAGHETTI
CAMPANELLE	GIGLI	STROZZAPRETI
CANNELLONI	GOMITI	TAGLIATELLE
CAVATELLI	MANICOTTI	TORTELLINI
CENCIONI	PENNE	TORTIGLIONI
CONCHIGLIE	RIGATONI	TRENNE
DITALINI	ROTINI	TRIPOLINE
FARFALLE	SAGNARELLI	VERMICELLI

PUZZLE 142: EGYPTIAN PHARAOHS

```
N N E R I K A R E B N S Y U K
Y N R S E N A R M E R W S H T
U Y A E E T F E F A M H H S A
S U K B K N H E R E K R E R R
E S R K F R R K H U M A P N U
R E E A R E E K A E H D S S A
R R J Y F K E S K N A A E E K
E K T R N S H E D K A K S E N
I A E H P I E M P R H S K R E
N F N F A R F E D E J D A E M
I B T E E O T R M P K S F M I
E O H S A O K K E R A K R E M
H R O J H U H H U R E F E N S
R J E M E E A E A N E D J I B
D K I P T K R T K H O R A H A
```

ANEDJIB	MERKARE	SANAKHTE
DJEDEFRA	NARMER	SEBKAY
DJOSER	NEFEREFRE	SEKHEMKHET
HOR-AHA	NERIKARE	SEMERKHET
HOTEPSEKHEMWY	NETJERKARE	SHEPSESKAF
IMHOTEP	NYUSERRE INI	SNEFERU
MENKAURA	SAHURE	USERKAF

PUZZLE 143: FORESTS

```
N C E A A G T S A N N A V A S
M O W W N E E M A N G R O V E
O N T P E L U T A E P A B A T
I I W N V T C G M N D G O N O
S F T A E L L A I O L R R T C
T E A R O I Q A O R A S E A D
E R C U E U C W N I R T A I E
V O D O I S N N N D G A L G C
E U I S A E A F A A A T G A I
R S L T E S O E L O W L A N D
G A I R I R T L Z W O L A H U
R L G I E G E A R R C E T E O
E W O S L R A N L R A R R A U
E N T W Y O E P R A A V E T S
N M R I U L A R O T T I L H O
```

ANCIENT	GREENWOOD	PEAT
BOREAL	HEATH	RAINFOREST
CLOUD	IGAPO	SAVANNA
COASTAL	LITTORAL	SELVA
CONIFEROUS	LOWLAND	TAIGA
DECIDUOUS	MANGROVE	VARZEA
GALLERY	MAQUIS	WETLAND
GARRIGUE	MOIST EVERGREEN	

PUZZLE 144: SPY STUFF

```
E P R E O E O R S E C R E T S
S A H C O V E R R S L C O E A
O R T I S P Y M A S T E R R S
G E A V O O R O A T N O A G O
C E R E H P I C P D E R S A H
N A P D E D D A I G C M G N D
R O E E E A S R A O I E S E N
R M E A T S L N A O N O F O O
N E A S P T O Y V T I E P S I
L A L O P I E E T C R O I T
D P R D P I A R E T E L S L A
O T O S N T R S O R R L D H T
C A E R R A S R M P C V E E S
S E H E D A H C L E A N E R V
T A S P P R E E L O M V I S A
```

AGENT
ASSET
CIPHER
CLEANER
CODE
COVER
DEFECTOR
DEVICE
DROP

ESPIONAGE
HANDLER
MOLE
PASSPORT
SECRET
SPYMASTER
STATION
VISA

PUZZLE 145: FESTIVALS

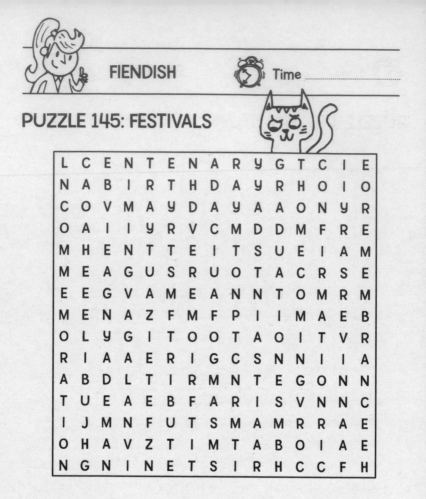

```
L C E N T E N A R Y G T C I E
N A B I R T H D A Y R H O I O
C O V M A Y D A Y A A O N Y R
O A I I Y R V C M D D M F R E
M H E N T T E I T S U E I A M
M E A G U S R U O T A C R S E
E E G V A M E A N N T O M R M
M E N A Z F M F P I I M A E B
O L Y G I T O O T A O I T V R
R I A A E R I G C S N N I I A
A B D L T I R M N T E G O N N
T U E A E B F A R I S V N N C
I J M N F U T S M A M R R A E
O H A V Z T I M T A B O I A E
N G N I N E T S I R H C C F H
```

ANNIVERSARY	CONFIRMATION	MARRIAGE
BAR MITZVAH	FETE	MAY DAY
BAT MITZVAH	FIRST COMMUNION	NAME DAY
BIRTHDAY	GALA	PARTY
CENTENARY	GRADUATION	REMEMBRANCE
CHRISTENING	HARVEST FESTIVAL	REUNION
COMING OF AGE	HOMECOMING	SAINT'S DAY
COMMEMORATION	JUBILEE	TRIBUTE

PUZZLE 146: TENNIS

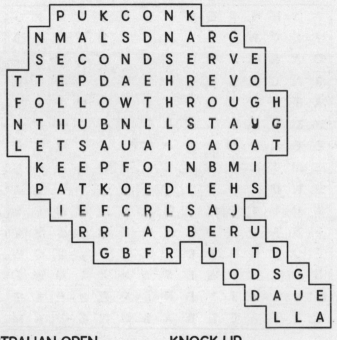

AUSTRALIAN OPEN	KNOCK UP
BALL-BOY	LADIES DOUBLES
BREAK	LET
DOUBLE FAULT	LINE JUDGE
DROP-SHOT	LOB
FIFTEEN	OVERHEAD
FOLLOW-THROUGH	RACKET
GAME	SECOND SERVE
GRAND SLAM	SET
GRIP	SMASH
HIT	

PUZZLE 147: AESOP'S FABLES

```
A S M E A G L E A N D F O X T
F L O W D E I R C O H W Y O B
O A E L B M A R B D N A R I F
X N O I L D N A X O F T N S A
A T H E A S T R O N O M E R S
N C R O W A N D P I T C H E R
D C N E M R E H S I F E H T C
G M I S C H I E V O U S D O G
R N G A B M A L D N A F L O W
A C L I O N A N D M O U S E M
P B A L D M A N A N D F L Y E
E D F H A F O X A N D C R O W
S M A N A N D S W A L L O W L
E R E P I V D N A R E M R A F
E E T A C D N A S U N E V A M
```

BALD MAN AND FLY
BOY WHO CRIED WOLF
CROW AND PITCHER
EAGLE AND FOX
FARMER AND VIPER
FIR AND BRAMBLE
FOX AND CROW
FOX AND GRAPES
FOX AND LION

LION AND MOUSE
MAN AND SWALLOW
MISCHIEVOUS DOG
THE ASTRONOMER
THE FISHERMEN
TORTOISE AND HARE
VENUS AND CAT
WOLF AND LAMB

PUZZLE 148: FAMOUS SHIPS

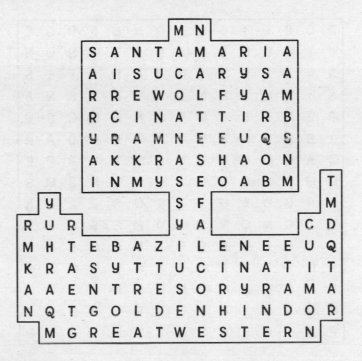

			M	N					
S	A	N	T	A	M	A	R	I	A
A	I	S	U	C	A	R	Y	S	A
R	R	E	W	O	L	F	Y	A	M
R	C	I	N	A	T	T	I	R	B
Y	R	A	M	N	E	E	U	Q	S
A	K	K	R	A	S	H	A	O	N
I	N	M	Y	S	E	O	A	B	M

BRITTANIC   QUEEN MARY
CUTTY SARK   SANTA MARIA
GOLDEN HIND   SYRACUSIA
GREAT WESTERN   TITANIC
MALTESE FALCON
MARY ROSE
MAYFLOWER
NOAH'S ARK
QUEEN ELIZABETH

PUZZLE 149: WEDDINGS

```
D D E D I I W V D V N E E G C
A I M U U B M R U H T A S U N
A V A S A V E T H E D A T E S
C I D M A S N S F I U N S N F
O R N R S I U F T N E R C G Y
L S B V R E U T H M E R C A R
O A N N I B D S N W A I A P E
U M M O A T O I O H S N S M S
R H B O I U A L R U S G R A B
S L G M O T F T M B E S G H E
C S O Y R R P S I S B S E C U
H O F E P A G E B O Y U M A C
E I T N H M V U C B N E I K U
M N H O I D I G R E M S O E I
E E I H A B S E V G R T T I E
```

BEST MAN	DRESS	MENU
BRIDESMAID	ENTERTAINMENT	MUSIC
BUFFET	FLOWERS	PAGEBOY
CAKE	GROOM	RECEPTION
CAR	GUEST LIST	RINGS
CHAMPAGNE	HONEYMOON	SAVE THE DATE
COLOUR SCHEME	INVITATIONS	VENUE

PUZZLE 150: AFTERNOON TEA

```
E H F O R K K T E R G A I M F
M P C T L C U R T A L C P C Y
A Y L I T D N A T S E K A C L
F G M A W T E A S P O O N K L
F U L A T D M K E G U H I R R
N T N R E E N G A P M A H C C
L R L S E R I A L C E Y C Y P
T N K U C C L S O Y P E A T
O W C M L O U H E N E R N T K
I D B T T O P A F T G A I M N
R N B U E N O C S L M A F A I
E E C C T S F G R S A C L J F
E A J I D T T A L K A T M I E
O E W A I T E R P E T M Y A C
E C K F A N A R K C P S L C U
```

BUTTER	JAM	TEASPOON
CAKE STAND	KNIFE	WAITER
CREAM	MENU	
CUP OF TEA	MILK	
EARL GREY	PLATE	
ECLAIR	SANDWICH	
FAIRY CAKE	SAUCER	
FINE CHINA	SCONE	
FORK	TEAPOT	

FIENDISH   Time ....

PUZZLE 151: MONSTERS

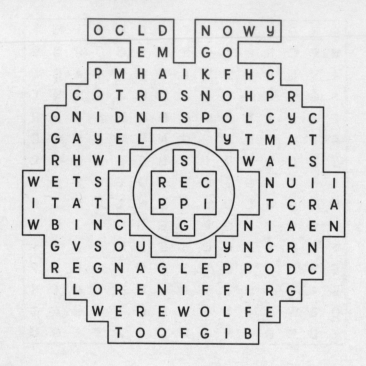

```
O C L D   N O W Y
    E M   G O
  P M H A I K F H C
  C O T R D S N O H P R
O N I D N I S P O L C Y C
G A Y E L     Y T M A T
R H W I   S   W A L S
W E T S  R E C  N U I I
I T A T  P P I  T C R A
W B I N C  G   N I A E N
G V S O U     Y N C R N
  R E G N A G L E P P O D C
  L O R E N I F F I R G
    W E R E W O L F E
      T O O F G I B
```

BASILISK   MANTICORE
BIGFOOT   MINOTAUR
CYCLOPS   OGRE
DEMON   SIREN
DOPPELGANGER   TYPHON
DRACULA   WENDIGO
GRIFFIN   WEREWOLF
HYDRA   WRAITH
LEVIATHAN

PUZZLE 152: CHRISTMAS CAROLS

```
P  L  R  W  E  X  F  O  R  D  C  A  R  O  L
W  O  C  H  R  I  S  T  M  A  S  T  R  E  E
A  M  T  H  E  F  I  R  S  T  N  O  E  L  E
S  L  L  E  B  E  H  T  F  O  L  O  R  A  C
S  R  H  T  S  I  L  E  N  T  N  I  G  H  T
A  T  H  E  H  U  R  O  N  C  A  R  O  L  F
I  E  J  O  Y  T  O  T  H  E  W  O  R  L  D
L  N  B  L  U  E  C  H  R  I  S  T  M  A  S
W  J  I  N  G  L  E  B  E  L  L  R  O  C  K
A  O  H  O  L  Y  N  I  G  H  T  A  T  I  E
S  T  W  A  E  L  B  V  O  B  T  E  A  J  A
S  T  A  W  A  Y  I  N  A  M  A  N  G  E  R
A  L  O  R  A  C  Y  R  T  N  E  V  O  C  I
I  S  S  I  L  V  E  R  B  E  L  L  S  P  V
L  D  A  D  I  V  A  N  Z  I  L  E  F  R  U
```

AWAY IN A MANGER
BLUE CHRISTMAS
CAROL OF THE BELLS
COVENTRY CAROL
FELIZ NAVIDAD
JINGLE-BELL ROCK
JOY TO THE WORLD
O CHRISTMAS TREE
O HOLY NIGHT
SILENT NIGHT

SILVER BELLS
THE FIRST NOEL
THE HURON CAROL
UP ON THE HOUSETOP
WASSAIL WASSAIL
WEXFORD CAROL

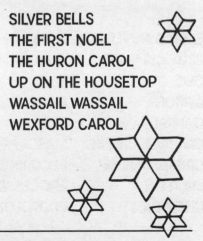

PUZZLE 153: CHEESES

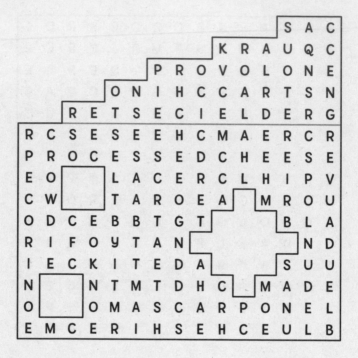

```
                                    S A C
                              K R A U Q C
                        P R O V O L O N E
                    O N I H C C A R T S N
                R E T S E C I E L D E R G
R C S E S E E H C M A E R C R
P R O C E S S E D C H E E S E
E O     L A C E R C L H I P V
C W     T A R O E A   M R O U
O D C E B B T G T     B L A
R I F O Y T A N       N D
I E C K I T E D A     S U U
N     N T M T D H C   M A D E
O     O M A S C A R P O N E L
E M C E R I H S E H C E U L B
```

BLEU D'AUVERGNE
BLUE CHESHIRE
BRIE
CABOC
CANTAL
COTTAGE CHEESE
CREAM CHEESE
CROTTIN
CROWDIE

DERBY
DUNLOP
EDAM
EMMENTALER
FETA
MASCARPONE
PECORINO
PROCESSED CHEESE
PROVOLONE

QUARK
RED LEICESTER
STRACCHINO

PUZZLE 154: FAIRGROUND

```
Y H S T U N O C O C P F J S E
E A T L W Z M H L O J D L L G
F U N R A L E O T U N E P O E
U N E E L U W G G U E P C T Y
N T M T T N I G O H A A R M D
H E E S Z B L R W E R I E V U
O D S A E E O S E O D G S C J
U H U O R G I F U E D N T H D
S O M C Y R F S S O R N A I N
E U A R R O E V D M T U L N A
R S R E T L E K S R E T L E H
R E F L C A N D Y F L O S S C
M E H L E G H O S T T R A I N
G E B O T U O B A D N U O R U
S C A R N I V A L E M U L F P
```

AMUSEMENTS   FERRIS WHEEL   PUNCH AND JUDY
BIG TOP   FLUME   RIDES
CANDYFLOSS   FUNHOUSE   ROLLER COASTER
CARNIVAL   GHOST TRAIN   ROUNDABOUT
CAROUSEL   HAUNTED HOUSE   SLOT MACHINES
CLOWN   HELTER-SKELTER   STALLS
COCONUT SHY   JUGGLER   TOFFEE APPLE
DODGEM   MERRY-GO-ROUND   WALTZER

PUZZLE 155: TOYS

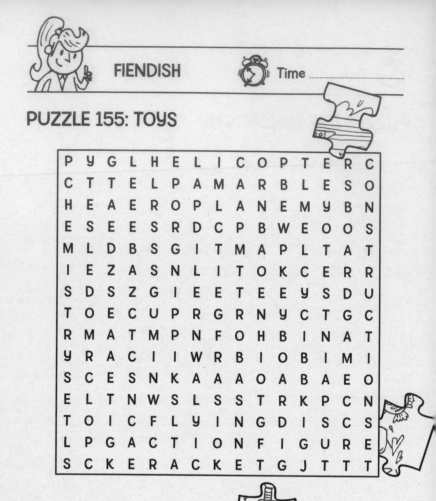

```
P Y G L H E L I C O P T E R C
C T T E L P A M A R B L E S O
H E A E R O P L A N E M Y B N
E S E E S R D C P B W E O O S
M L D B S G I T M A P L T A T
I E Z A S N L I T O K C E R R
S D S Z G I E E T E E Y S D U
T O E C U P R G R N Y C T G C
R M A T M P N F O H B I N A T
Y R A C I I W R B I O B I M I
S C E S N K A A A O A B A E O
E L T N W S L S S T R K P C N
T O I C F L Y I N G D I S C S
L P G A C T I O N F I G U R E
S C K E R A C K E T G J T T T
```

ACTION FIGURE	DOLL	MODEL SET
AEROPLANE	FLYING DISC	PAINT SET
BALL	FRISBEE	RACING CAR
BAT	HELICOPTER	RACKET
BICYCLE	JIGSAW PUZZLE	SKIPPING ROPE
BOARD GAME	KEYBOARD	SPINNING TOP
CHEMISTRY SET	KITE	WATER PISTOL
CONSTRUCTION SET	MARBLES	

PUZZLE 156: PENGUINS

```
R A C G R P I D D K H O U L T
G F H Y E R L H F A L E R O L
S R I K B H E M P L L N S K W
O I N O R A C A M T O O P O M
E C S E R A N S T H G Y L G N
G A T Y O D M I T A E R R N F
E N R M E G L D P M O O I I O
O M A G E L L A N I C R L K R
O M P N E O L L N K D E D E D
E L T C B A O O H D D P R E P
P O T M G M D O W A C M A L O
O A U R E L P O R E A E D R K
O H T P M P A E R O Y A L R E
D E T S E R C T C E R E F T E
A I Y R O P U A S A E H D I O
```

ADELIE   KING

AFRICAN   LITTLE

CHINSTRAP   MACARONI

EMPEROR   MAGELLANIC

ERECT-CRESTED   ROCKHOPPER

FIORDLAND   ROYAL

GALAPAGOS   SNARES

GENTOO   YELLOW-EYED

HUMBOLDT

PUZZLE 157: EXTINCT ANIMALS

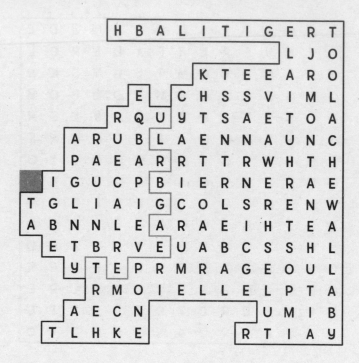

AUROCH

BALI TIGER

BLUEBUCK

EMPEROR RAT

IMPOSTER HUTIA

JAVAN TIGER

LESSER BILBY

MONTANE HUTIA

ORIENTE CAVE RAT

QUAGGA

SEA MINK

TARPAN

THYLACINE

TOOLACHE WALLABY

TULE SHREW

PUZZLE 158: BISCUITS

```
R T R F O L E E R I P M E D Z
O I E V I T S E G I D K R A V
F D K D L C R K I S A I D O R
S M A C A R O O N C D E N O F
G D C E K S P T T D A T K I R
T M A E R C D R A T S U C R T
R B F E P B O E E L R N A S S
O I F R R H R Z B D A R J R I
L A A I S B B E T E O E P K B
W A J B T E P P G A E G A E O
I K A R R L G S T N M N L U U
B A O A E T H C I R I I F E R
T H B I D L A B I R A G C R B
S M N R E K C A R C C I R P O
B H P R E T Z E L I N C O L N
```

BOURBON
CRACKER
CRISPBREAD
CUSTARD CREAM
DIGESTIVE
EMPIRE
FLAPJACK
GARIBALDI
GINGERBREAD

GINGER NUT
JAFFA CAKE
LINCOLN
MACAROON
MATZO
NICE
OATCAKE
PRETZEL
RICH TEA

SHORTBREAD
SHORTCAKE
WAFER

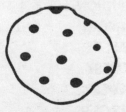

PUZZLE 159: GEOLOGY

```
E F N S A E G R A S S L A N D
T O T L I S T R I V E R B E D
V R R O A C D H G Y C N J O R
L E A R J N A S I H E R L T G
S S O A U A E N I Y E L L A V
I T P T G R M P Y I L P D L N
M E A D O W E V C O G E N S D
T P N L C L S A V A N N A H E
L P O N A C L O V F U I L O L
E E S G V G G C D A J N S T T
N F O T E O M N I V A S I M R
L I E Y R R N I A T N U O M E
O M S G N E T I T C A L A T S
I E E V L L A F R E T A W S E
R T W I S A R M T D L W F E D
```

ARCHIPELAGO
CANYON
CAVERN
DESERT
FOREST
GEYSER
GLACIER
GORGE
GRASSLAND
ISLAND

JUNGLE
MEADOW
MOUNTAIN
PENINSULA
RIVERBED
SAVANNAH
STALACTITE
STALAGMITE
STEPPE
STREAM

TUNDRA
VALLEY
VOLCANO
WATERFALL

PUZZLE 160: DESERTS

```
A A P L A R O T N N T N M S N
M I R C E N R N A S K G N N M
A G R Y D N A S T A E R G U T
C R H A T Y N M L M N E K B A
A E I N G O I A I N A A A I E
T A Z V S N II V A B R T Y A N
A T A P A A U H R A O B S N A
Y V M A R K S Z K B N A I R I
D I M I P A M E D N O S L O B
S C N N L M O R D O S I C A A
R T P A T A G O N I A N N O R
A O A I A L A D K A P T E B A
I R D R I K Y Z Y L K U M N H
Y I B Y N A U H A U H I H C A
M A A S I T R U T S U Y D R S
```

ALASHAN	KALAHARI	SONORAN
ARABIAN	KARA-KUM	SYRIAN
ATACAMA	KAVIR	TAKLA MAKAN
BET-PAK-DALA	KYZYL-KUM	UST-URT
BOLSON DE MAPIMI	NAMIB	
CHIHUAHUAN	NUBIAN	
DZUNGARIA	ORDOS	
GREAT BASIN	PATAGONIAN	
GREAT SANDY	SAHARA	
GREAT VICTORIA	SIMPSON	

PUZZLE 161: SPACECRAFT

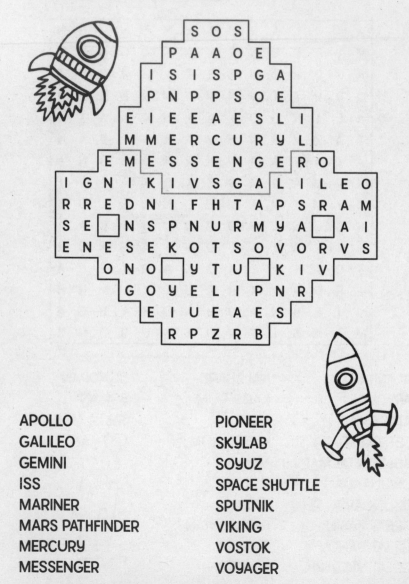

APOLLO	PIONEER
GALILEO	SKYLAB
GEMINI	SOYUZ
ISS	SPACE SHUTTLE
MARINER	SPUTNIK
MARS PATHFINDER	VIKING
MERCURY	VOSTOK
MESSENGER	VOYAGER

ALL THE ANSWERS

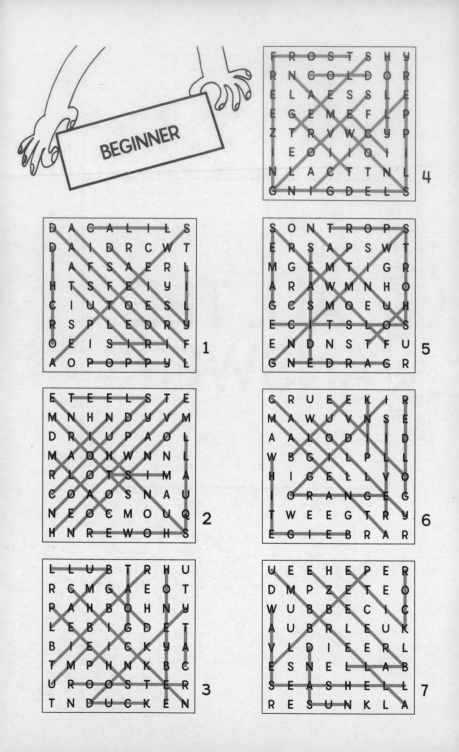

BEGINNER

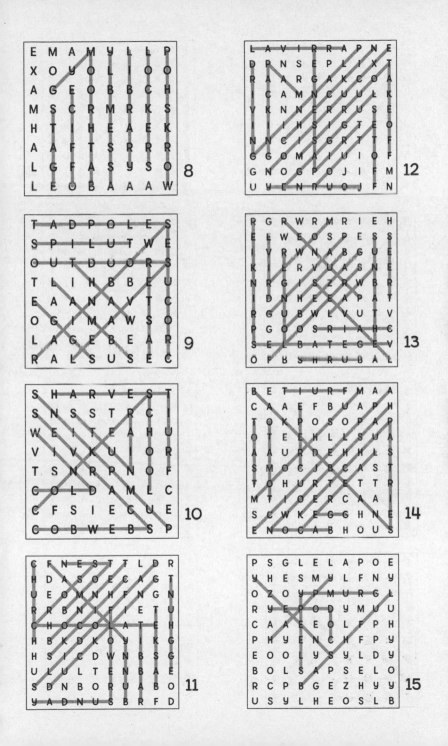

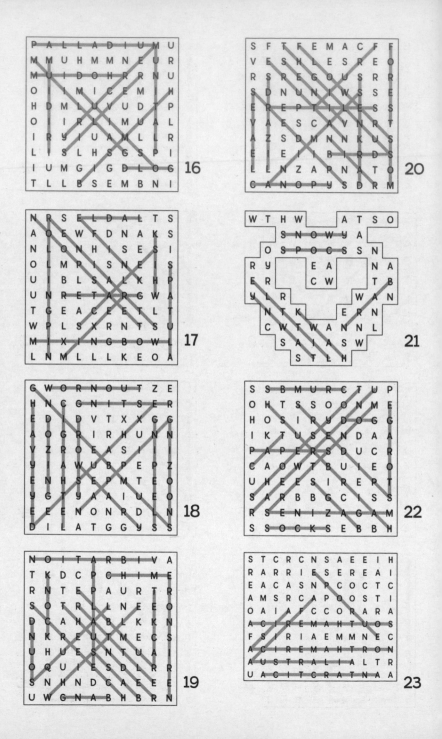

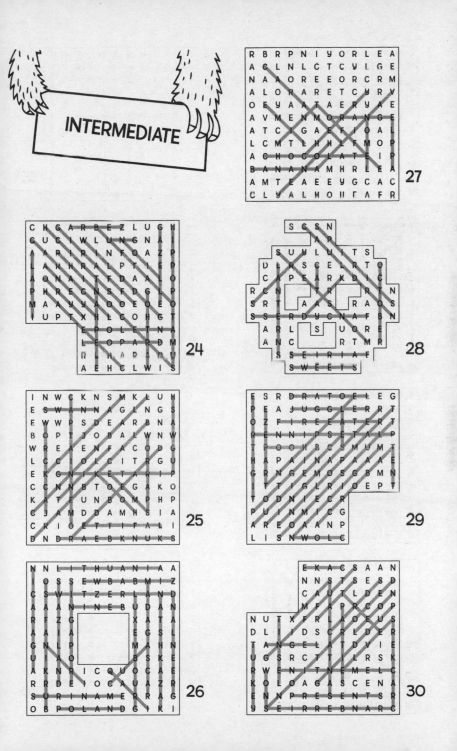

INTERMEDIATE

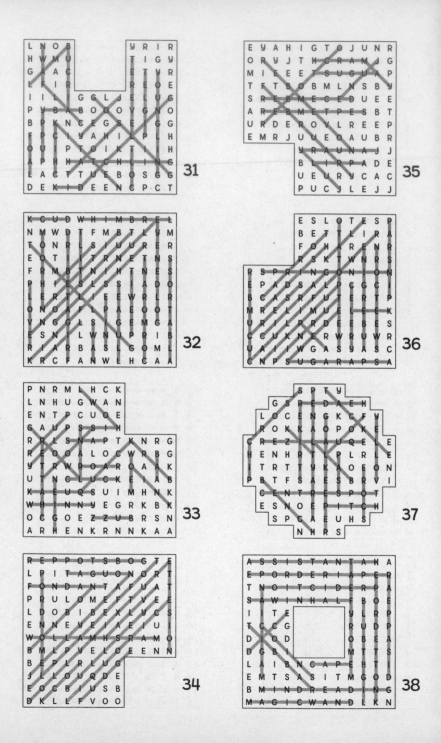

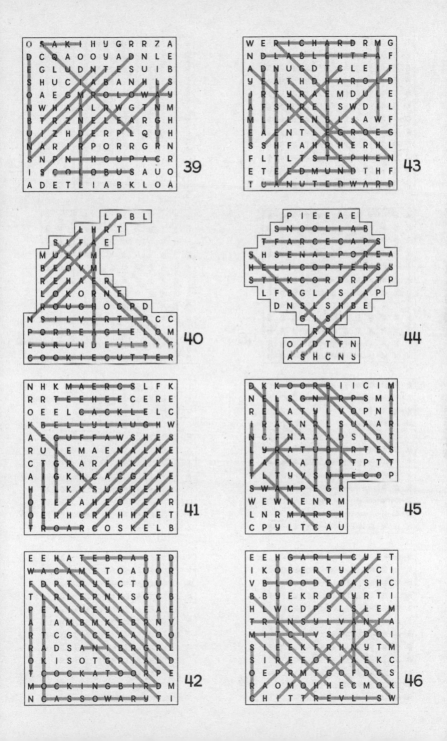

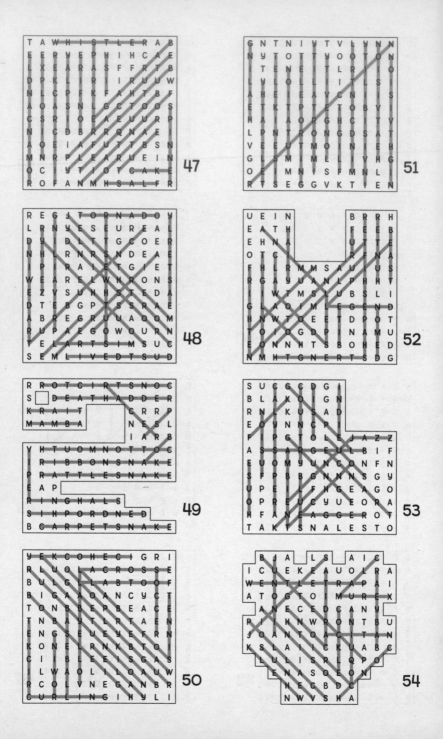

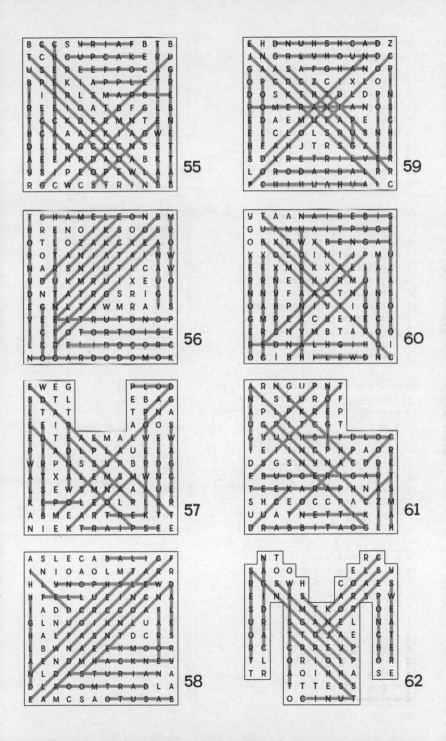

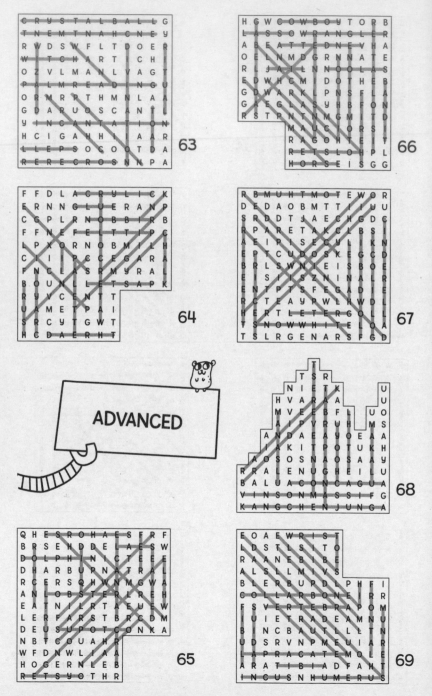

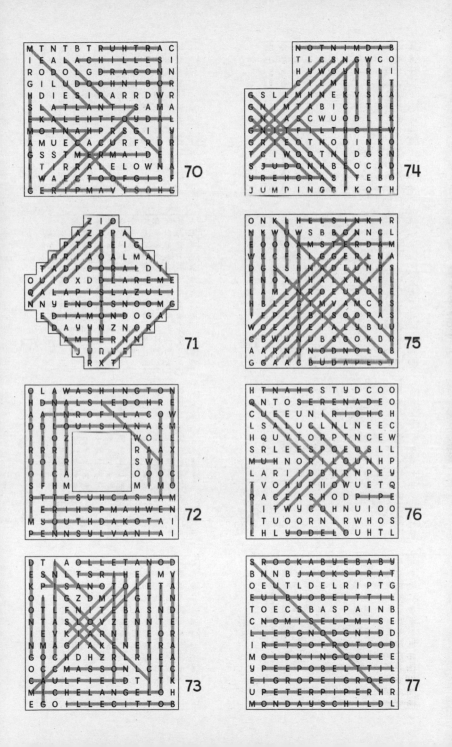

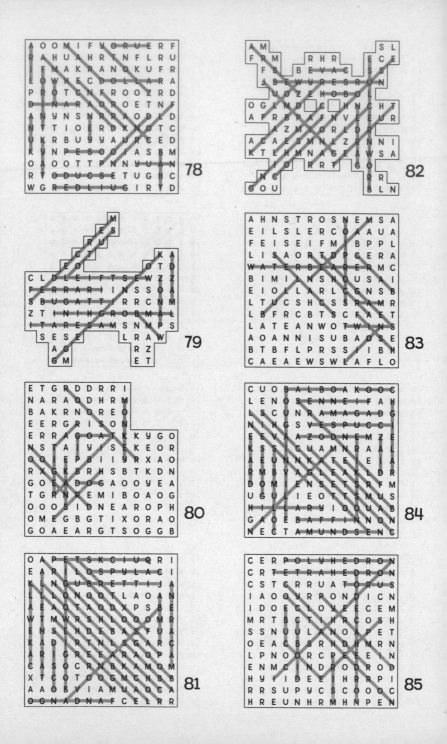

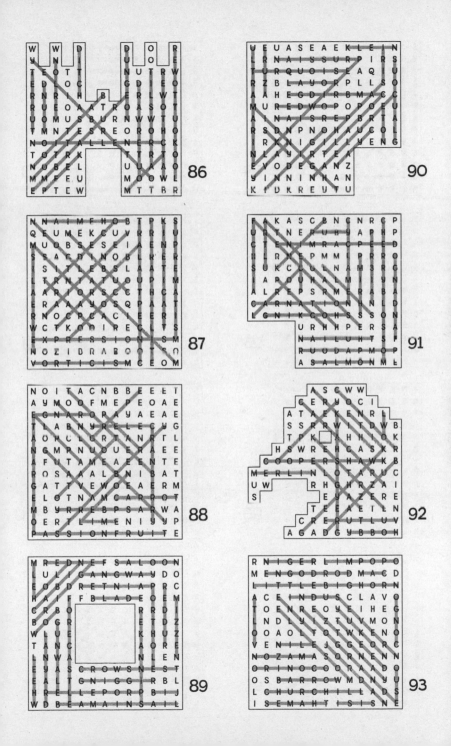

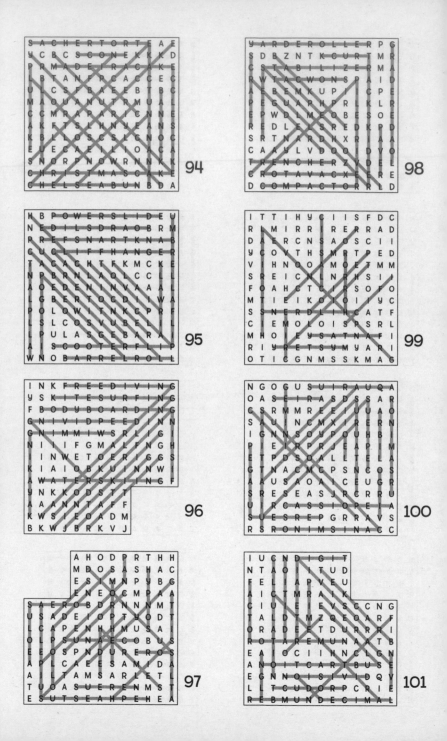

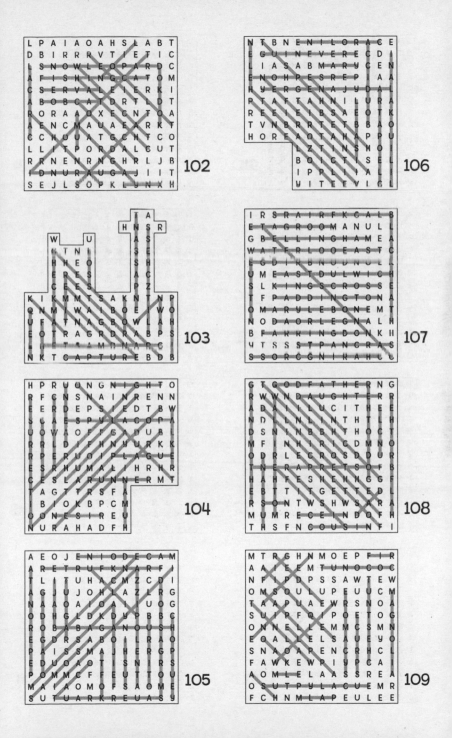

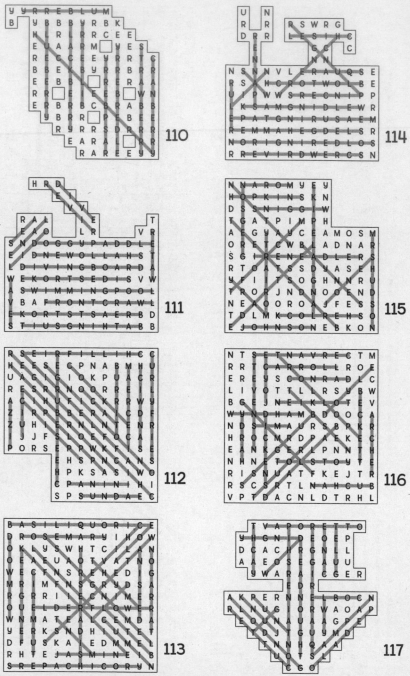

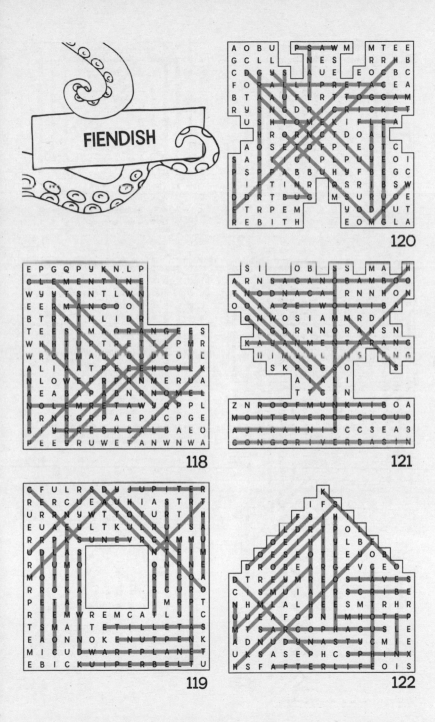

FIENDISH

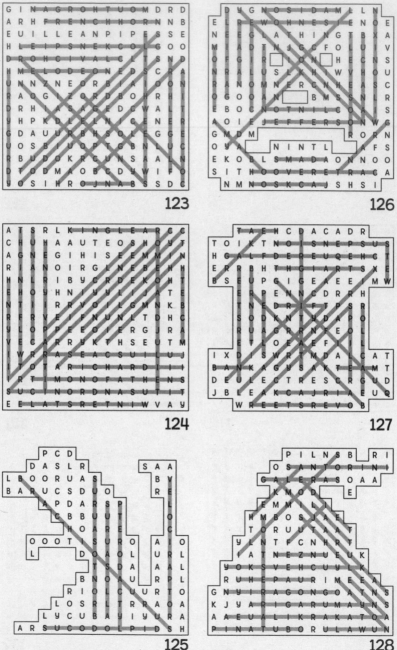

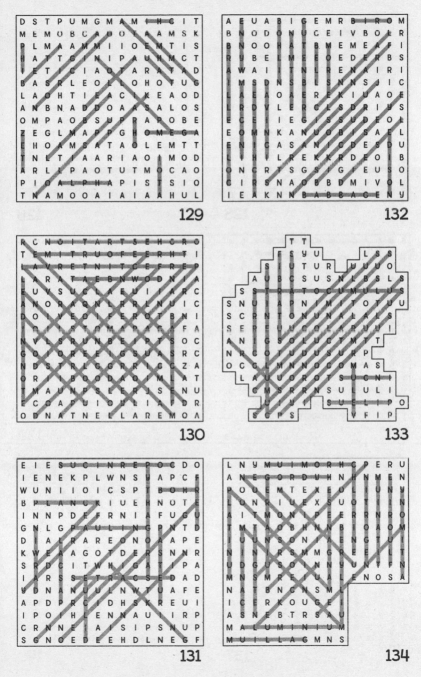

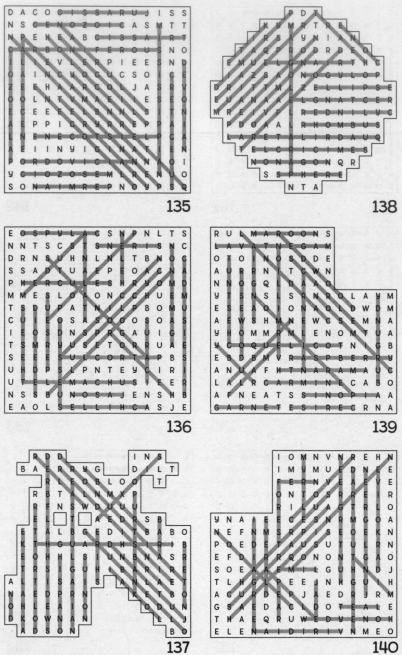

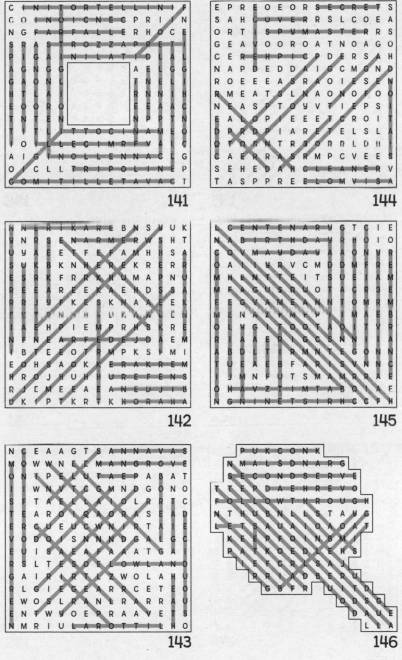

141

144

142

145

143

146

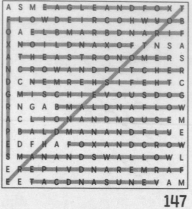

147

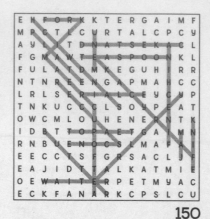

150

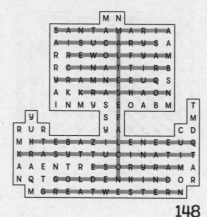

148

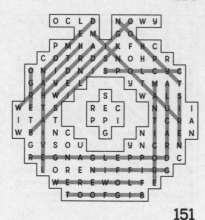

151

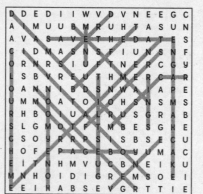

149

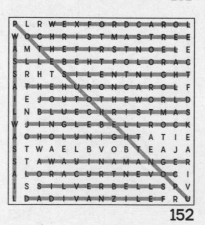

152

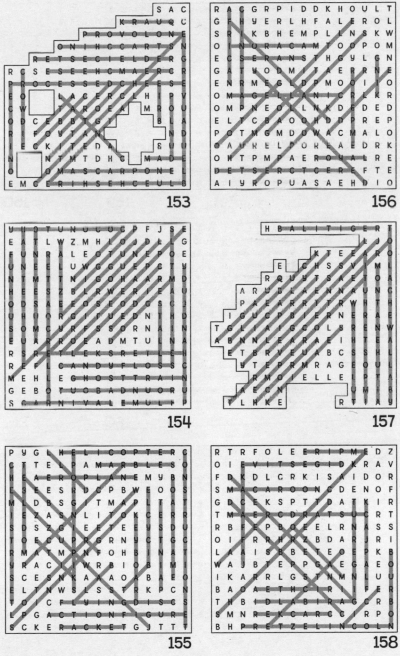

153

156

154

157

155

158

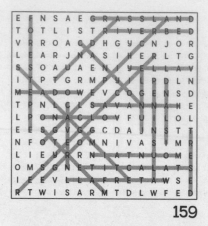

```
E F N S A E G R A S S L A N D
T O T L I S T R I V E R B E D
V R R O A C D H G Y C N J O R
L E A R J N A S I H E R L T G
S S O A U A E N Y E L L A V
I T P T G R M P V P D L N
M E A D O W E V C O G E N S D E
T P N L G L S A V A N N A H E
L P O N A C L O V F U I L O L
E E S G V G C D A J N S T T
N F O T E O M N I V A S I M R
L I E U R R N I A T N U O M E
O M S G N E T I C A L A T S
I E E V L L A F R E T A W S E
R T W I S A R M T D L W F E D
```

159

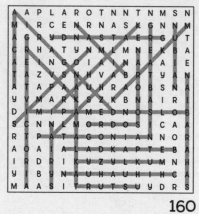

```
A A P L A R O T N N T N M S N
M I R C E N R N A S K G N N M
A G R U D N A S T A E R G U T A
C R H A T U N M L M N E K B A E
A E I N G O I A N A A I Y A N
T A P A U H V A B R T Y A N A
Y V M A R K S Z K B N A I R I
D I M I P A M E D N O S L O B
S C N N L M O R D O S I C A A
R T P A T A G O N I A N N O R A
A O A I A L A D K A P T E B A
I R D R I K U Z U L K U M N
Y I B Y N A U H A U H I H C A
M A A S I T R U T S U Y D R S
```

160

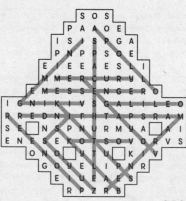

```
        S O S
      P A A O E
    I S I S P G A
    P N P P S O E
  E I E E A E S L I
  M M E R C U R Y L
  E M E S S E N G E R O
I G N I K I V S G A L I L E O
R R E D N I F H T A P S R A M
S E   N S P N U R M Y A   A I
E N E S E K O   S O V O R V S
  O N O   Y T U   K   V
  G O Y E L I P N R
    E I U E A E S
      R P Z R B
```

161